Your To Be List

Your To Be List

Turn Those Dreaded To-Do's
Into Meaningful Moments
Every Day

Lauren Rosenfeld & James McMahon

WISDOMOLOGY PUBLISHING

To our parents, who opened our eyes to wonder.
And our children, who show us new wonders every day.

WISDOMOLOGY PUBLISHING
Published by Wisdomology, LLC, Asheville, NC 28801

Copyright ©2010 Lauren Rosenfeld and James McMahon

Cover art by Patrick Scully
Cover design by Patrick Scully
Interior design and page composition by shu shu design

The authors and publisher of this book do not dispense medical, health, financial or other advice. Should you choose to use any of the ideas in the book, the author and publisher assume no responsibility for your actions.

To Be List™ is a Trademark of Wisdomology, LLC.

Wisdomology® is a Registered Trademark of Wisdomology, LLC.

ISBN-13: 978-0-9843207-0-7
ISBN-10: 0-9843207-0-9
Category: Self-Help, Personal Growth, Self-improvement

1st printing, January 2010

Contents

Preface

"We need to practice... gently but steadily, throughout our daily life, not wasting a single opportunity or event to look deeply into the nature of life, including our everyday problems. Practicing this way, we dwell in profound communion with life."

— ZEN MASTER THICH NHAT HANH

"Know that every deed counts; that every word is power. Above all, remember that despite all absurdities and all frustrations and all disappointments, the meaning of life is to build your life as if it were a work of art."

— RABBI ABRAHAM JOSHUA HESCHEL

When was the last time you leaned back, stretched your arms wide, beamed your biggest smile, and sighed with pleasure, "Yes, this is what life's all about"?

We all have different answers. Maybe you were gazing at a sunset over the ocean with your beloved. Or maybe you were playing checkers with a grandchild. Or sitting in a fishing boat on a perfect summer morning. Cooking dinner on a Saturday night with your kids. Driving on the open road with the windows down and your favorite song booming through the car's speakers. Perhaps you were quietly writing in your journal on the couch in your living room while sipping a cup of hot tea.

Whatever your answer, the "*this*" that "life's all about" has to do with a sense of deep communion with life. Perhaps you were communing with nature—or a loved one. Perhaps you were even communing with some deep sense of who you truly are. Whatever it was, you were sensing that you are part of something greater than yourself. You were not feeling "myself-against-the-world," but "myself-with-the world."

The emotions you had when you felt that life was flowing in just the right way were probably feelings of love, contentment, relaxation, joy, and inspiration.

These moments are like gifts to our souls. They refresh us, energize us, and give us a sense of deeper purpose. They remind us that the meaning of our lives is alive, vital, and humming just beneath the surface of our experience.

Of course, there are also times when life *does* seem absurd. Meaningless. And frustrating. And disappointing. We might find ourselves consumed by boredom, worry, or despair. At difficult moments like these, it may seem like those deeply meaningful *what-life's-all-about* moments were nothing more than happy accidents: strokes of blind luck that can be enjoyed when they happen but which cannot be consciously recreated or repeated. They have a magical quality; but, like magic, they are outside of our control. Deep within, we long to regain that sense of deep communion. We want to feel that our lives are a canvas on which we paint the masterpiece of our lives.

Your To Be List is a system through which we can live with a deep sense of communion and meaning every moment of our lives, whether we are gazing out at a tropical sunset or a sea of traffic. Communion and meaning are always available. Like an artist who stands before a blank canvas, we just need to be trained to see the potential.

With *Your To Be List*, you will see that every moment has the potential to become a *what-life's-all-about* moment. We just have to learn to see the potential for deep connection with the meaning of life in each and every situation. We *can* build our lives as if they were works of art. *Your To Be List* will show you how. And you will see that the choice to engage with meaning is your choice to make every moment of your life. What's more, you will see that when you are engaged with meaning, your words and your actions have the power to transform your life and your world for the better.

- **Part One** of this book explains just what *Your To Be List* is, why it is important and just how to build it. We give you step-by-step instructions about how to create *Your To Be List* and how to use it to help you stay constantly oriented toward the meaning in your life. The steps are remarkably easy to follow and can immediately be integrated into your daily routine.
- **Part Two** is our personal story of how living in alignment with the energies of *Your To Be List* transformed our lives and the life of our family forever. The story is written by Lauren and is told in her voice. However, the story itself belongs to both of us, belongs to all of us. And we hope that it will inspire you to create your own To Be List story that resonates with deep feeling and profound meaning.
- **Part Three** brings *Your To Be List* to life by giving you simple, yet powerful exercises for practicing your "To Be's." Every time you read through the chapters and the exercises, you'll strengthen your ability to live *Your To Be List* from day to day and moment to moment.

    You can read through these exercises in order or you can flip through them, finding just the exercise you need in the moment. Even if you only have time to look at one exercise in the middle of your day, you'll be connecting to the deepest meaning in your life, building your strength to bring that meaning into every moment through Your To Be List, and healing yourself on a subtle, yet deep level.

    These simple, refreshing exercises are there to help you practice *Your To Be List*, even (and especially) when you are having trouble connecting to the meaning and joy in your life.

We hope that you will return to this book again and again; that you will reread the sections, sampling them as you need the inspiration. We hope that you will rely upon your wisdom and your deep knowing to help you find the section of this book that will benefit you most in the moment.

We also hope that you will find this book to be a blessing in your life— and that the work of art that is your life will continue *To Be* a blessing to everyone you meet.

— JAMES MCMAHON AND LAUREN ROSENFELD

Part One:
What *is* Your
To Be List?

It's morning. The house is still dark.

I lumber downstairs to make my morning coffee. I flip on the kitchen light, reach for a coffee mug—and then I see it. Sitting on the counter top. Imposing and menacing.

"Wash the car!" *it tells me.* **"Go to the bank! Take the kids to soccer! Fold the wash! Call Mom! E-mail meeting agenda before 9:00! Pay the bills!"**

I close my eyes and try willing it to go away. This can't be happening. Not yet. All I want is a moment of peace, a moment to breathe in the day's possibilities. I want to greet this day with joy. Can't it let me be? Just this once?

I open one bleary eye. **"Go to the grocery store!"** *it commands. I rub my temples and try to remain calm. The day hasn't yet started and I am already exhausted by its demands.*

It's my to-do list. To the naked eye, nothing more than a simple slip of lined paper whose contents are written in my very own handwriting. It's certainly nothing to be afraid of. But the mere sight of it makes me want to turn around and go right back to bed.

Do you have a to-do list? Most of us do. Maybe yours is neatly detailed in the pages of a leather-bound planner. Maybe it is scrawled haphazardly on the backs of several grocery receipts that are lying at the bottom of your purse. Perhaps it is entered precisely into your handheld electronic calendar. Or maybe it is written on dozens of brightly colored sticky notes that are scattered across your desk like confetti. It's even possible your to-do list is nothing more than a constant mental tally of your ongoing commitments and responsibilities.

No matter what it looks like, or where it resides, take a moment right now to think about your to-do list.

How do you feel when you glance at it at the start of each day? Uplifted? Eager? Joyful?

Probably not.

Most of us look at our to-do lists and immediately feel quite the opposite: we scan this seemingly endless inventory of tasks and are suddenly struck with feelings of pressure, anxiety, and exhaustion. Physically, we might even get a sinking sensation in our hearts or a queasy feeling in our guts. We may look at our to-do lists at the start of the day and draw a deep breath into our lungs to overcome the overwhelming sensation that we are drowning in a sea of deadlines, appointments, phone calls, meetings, and errands.

Yet, despite these uneasy feelings, we can hardly imagine our lives without our to-do lists. They help to keep our lives on track. They help us remember our priorities, promises, and commitments by setting them out in clear view. They help keep us organized and accountable. At the same time, however, they are constant reminders of our overcommitted, thinly stretched, demanding lives. Every day, we look at our to-do lists and we ask ourselves this eternal, plaintive question:

"How will I ever get it all done?"

To-do lists tend to drain our energy. And it's no wonder. The tasks on our lists usually feel cut off from the deeper meaning of our lives—the meaning that feeds our souls and makes us feel joyful and hopeful. A typical to-do list includes items like "drop off the cleaning," "take the dog to the groomer," or "invoice clients." As we cross these items off our lists we may wonder, "Is this what I was put on earth to do?"

For most of us, the answer is a clear, resounding "No!" These tasks feel like nothing more than time-consuming, mind-numbing distractions from our real life's work of fulfilling our soul's purpose.

In fact, we instinctively have the sense that if we can just get to the bottom of that darned list, and check off the last item, we will finally be free. Free to put aside meaningless distractions and dive into the deeper, more meaningful parts of our lives—the parts that sweetly beckon us from beneath the surface of all the mundane daily details.

It seems to make sense: get the meaningless tasks out of the way, and then luxuriate in the meaningful experience of life that ultimately awaits us.

However, there are a couple of deep flaws in this thinking. The first problem is that we are effectively putting meaningful experience last on our list. Is that really where it belongs?

The second flaw is even more troubling: Because there is no end to your to-do list (let's be honest, for every task we cross off, we write two more down), we will never get to the bottom of the list. We will never get to the meaningful experience we long for. We will forever forsake the meaningful for the meaningless. It's no way to live!

But there is another way, a way that does not force you to choose between daily life and meaningful living. It's called *Your To Be List*, and it merges daily living and meaningful existence in a way that will bring joy and fulfillment to each and every day.

When you look at *Your To Be List* at the start of each day, you *will* feel uplifted. You *will* feel eager to move through your day, because your daily tasks will shimmer with the light of meaning.

How do we begin? We begin by changing the first question we ask ourselves each day. We usually begin the day by asking, "What do I need to *do* today?" But there is a more essential question that we must ask ourselves instead—and that question is:

"What do I want TO BE today?"

So, What Exactly *Is* a "To Be"?

A "To Be" is like a lens through which we view and experience everything in our lives.

Imagine your alarm clock wakes you up one rainy morning. In your bedside table you have a drawer full of lenses (the kind you might imagine Sherlock Holmes carrying, with a long handle and a large, round looking glass). On one side of the drawer are the negative lenses: Be angry. Be resentful. Be impatient. Be worried. Be bitter. And so on.

On the other side of the drawer are the positive lenses: Be happy. Be grateful. Be loving. Be kind. Be honest. Be open.

You have a choice as to which lens you will pick up and use to look at your world.

Let's say you pick up the lens that is labeled "Be worried." Looking through this lens, everything you see fills you with fear and dread. You look up at the ceiling and wonder if the roof is going to start leaking, and you suddenly find yourself worrying about where you would find the money for such a repair if it were to happen. Listening to the downpour, you wonder if there is going to be terrible traffic as you drive to work. You look at the clock and are gripped by fear that you are going to be late for your morning meeting. You try to still your racing heart as you imagine your boss nervously tapping her fingers on the table, her eyes shifting between the conference room door and her watch. You worry about what might happen to you and your family if you lose your job. You haven't even put your feet on the floor and already your stomach is in a tight knot.

Okay. Now put away that nasty "Be worried" lens. It's not very useful, is it? Have a look on the other side of the drawer. Which lens would help you start your day joyfully, peacefully, and with compassion towards yourself?

Let's try picking up the "Be grateful" lens. It's the same rainy morning, but through this lens, you are able to see the blessings that rain brings.

You notice the rain falling on the lawn, watering your flowers, giving life to the trees. Perhaps you hear the sound of the rain on the roof and feel soothed by its natural rhythm. Looking next to you, perhaps you see the sleeping figure of your beloved. Maybe you hear the gentle snores of your children down the hall. You feel so fortunate to have this house that shelters you on this cozy, rainy morning. And not only that, you have a car that can take you to work. And in it you can stay dry. And miracle of miracles: you can listen to the music that you love, even if you are stuck behind traffic. And you've got this amazing little contraption called a cell phone, from which you can alert the office that you are running late. Your life is full of wonder and good fortune. You swing your feet out of bed and smile. Who could ask for a better morning?

Most people live their lives believing that circumstances dictate how they view the world. At some unconscious level they think, "The world has given me great cause to be fearful and worried. So I am naturally fearful and worried as a result. If the world gave me something to feel grateful about, I would feel grateful. But right now, I don't see anything to feel grateful for, so I don't feel grateful."

But *Your To Be List* is based on the very opposite premise: If you choose to be worried, your mind will go hunting for reasons to be worried, and you will most assuredly find them. The same is true for gratitude: If you choose to be grateful, your eyes will be open to the wonders of the world, and reasons to be grateful will come pouring into your heart.

So your "To Be's" are these powerful lenses through which we see the world. *And you get to choose which lenses you will see the world through.* That is how you will get started writing Your To Be List.

To Be Or Not To Be: What Exactly Goes On The List?

Now you need to ask yourself an important question: What do I want to get good at in my life?

Do you want to be more patient? More loving? Do you want to be happy? Relaxed? Creative? If you had a drawer full of lenses to choose from, which would you choose?

Another way to look at this is to ask yourself, "Ideally, how would I like people to describe me?" If two mutual friends ran into one another at the store or the water cooler, how would you like for them to finish this sentence:

"I really admire [your name here] because s/he is always so [your To Be's here]!"

The words you write in those blanks will become the first *To Be's* on *Your To Be List*!

To help get you started, here are ten basic "To Be's:"

* BE FREE
* BE HAPPY
* BE PEACEFUL
* BE LOVING
* BE STRONG
* BE BALANCED
* BE COURAGEOUS
* BE GRATEFUL
* BE BOUNTIFUL
* BE HEALING

Each of these ten basic "To Be's" head up a family of related "To Be's." Have a look at these "To Be" families and ask yourself which you would like to become good at.

So here (without further ado) are your choices of "To Be's":

Be Free—or Be Open, Be Limitless, Be Playful, Be Radiant, Be Laughing, Be Spirited, Be Bright, Be Gentle, Be Agile, Be Light-hearted

Be Happy—or Be Joyful, Be Blissful, Be Wise, Be Insightful, Be Inspired, Be Creative, Be Celebratory

Be Peaceful—or Be Relaxed, Be Knowing, Be Understanding, Be Harmonious, Be Serene, Be Still, Be Calm

Be Loving—or Be Giving, Be Nurturing, Be Caring, Be Devoted, Be Warm, Be Kind, Be Affectionate, Be Attentive

Be Strong—or Be Discerning, Be Ethical, Be Solid, Be Responsible, Be Decisive, Be Prudent, Be Honorable, Be Trustworthy

Be Balanced—or Be Beautiful, Be Stable, Be Poised, Be Even-tempered

Be Courageous—or Be Patient, Be Enduring, Be Assertive, Be Confident, Be Expressive, Be Trusting

Be Grateful—or Be Prayerful, Be Sincere, Be Yielding, Be Full of Awe, Be Releasing

Be Bountiful—or Be Abundant, Be Prosperous, Be Generous, Be Manifesting, Be Successful, Be Flourishing, Be Intentional, Be Blessed

Be Healing—or Be Whole, Be Complete, Be Compassionate, Be Patient, Be Helpful, Be Forgiving

Right now, choose your five top "To Be's" and write them down here:

1.
2.
3.
4.
5.

Now you have your basic *To Be List*! Wasn't that simple?

And, As For That Dreaded To-Do List...

So now that you have your "To Be's" for *Your To Be List*, does that mean that you toss your to-do list out the window?

Absolutely not! In order to complete *Your To Be List* you *need* your to-do's. In fact, without your to-do list, *Your To Be List* is nearly useless.

In the previous section, we asked you this question: "What do you want to get good at?"

Well, anything you want to get good at requires practice. If you want to get good at playing piano, you need to practice your scales. If you want to get good at golf, you need to practice your swing. If you want to get good at dancing, you need to practice your steps. Even people who are masters of their crafts had to begin with practice, and continue to practice diligently, in order to be the world-class talents we know them to be. LeBron James has to get out on the court with his teammates. Meryl Streep has to run her lines. Even the Dalai Lama meditates every day.

So in order to get good at our "To Be's" we need to practice. World Champion skater Michelle Kwan skates with an ethereal grace and athletic power that seems entirely effortless, but first she must warm up on the ice.

We cannot expect ourselves to move through our lives with power and grace without first warming up with our To Be's. Skating takes practice. So does happiness.

And this is exactly where those ever-present, never-ending to-do's come in handy. We use our to-do's to practice our "To Be's."

If you want to be happy, you don't need to wait for the next party to start. If you want to be relaxed, you don't need to go sit in solitude on an isolated beach. If you want to be creative, you don't have to sit down behind an easel. Being loving does not require candlelight, soft music, and a baby-sitter. And you certainly don't need to wait for a crisis to be compassionate and supportive.

If you didn't change a thing about your daily schedule or a single item on your to-do list, you would still have the opportunity to practice at being a happy, relaxed, creative, curious, and compassionate human being. In fact, once you learn how to use *Your To Be List*, you will find that you have multiple opportunities to practice at each and every one of these wonderful states of being each and every day.

Most of us bulldoze our way through our to-do list day after day, tending to our responsibilities, dispensing with phone calls, firing off E-mails, running errands, filing every last paper, and folding every last piece of laundry, so that we can finally put it all behind us when we get to that beach vacation we've been dreaming of. And oh, that beach vacation! We've seen it all in our heads thousands of times. The arcing stretch of soft, white sand. The feel of the sun and the breeze. The sound of the waves lapping against the shore. We imagine ourselves gazing out at the deep blue water and feeling entirely at peace. So we work efficiently and save religiously, and methodically cross off all our to-do's from our list.

And then the moment comes that we finally get to that beach. Everything is just as we imagined it would be: the sand, the sun, the breeze, the water, the waves. Yet, something is not right. Despite the lush and peaceful surroundings, despite our freedom from office meetings and household chores, we feel edgy and distracted. Our thoughts are flying in a thousand directions. We wonder what's going on back at work. We're worried about the kids. We're thinking about the contents of our bank accounts. We wonder if we should quickly check our E-mail or make a call home. Here we are on the beach vacation we dreamed of for so long, but our minds and our hearts are not on vacation.

We want to relax, we want to treasure the moment, but we don't know how. We haven't been practicing relaxation, so even when the perfect opportunity to relax has finally presented itself, we can't figure out what to do. It's like someone has handed us a violin for the first time and told us to play a Mozart concerto. We can't expect to be maestros of relaxation without first practicing our relaxation scales!

But if you live your life by *Your To Be List*, you will be practicing at being the relaxed person you want to be each and every single day, *while* you are making your way through your to-do list. By living your life by *Your To Be List*, you will find that when you do get to that beautiful beach and look out at the shimmering blue water, you will know how to be deeply relaxed, because you have been practicing being relaxed every day. In line at the grocery. While stuck in traffic. Walking the dog. Listening to hold music on the phone.

By living from *Your To Be List*, you will find that when you finally arrive at that water coloring class you have been yearning to take, and you sit down with your paint brush in your hand, you can truly let your creativity flow. You have been practicing at being creative while helping your kids with their homework or designing a more efficient office space at work.

Your To Be List will help you practice being loving while unloading the groceries with your beloved, so that when you finally do hire the babysitter for that long-awaited candlelit dinner, you will already have practiced at filling your heart with love and pouring it out generously for the person that deserves it most.

When you live by *Your To Be List*, you will find that when a friend or a family member comes to you in their time of need, you will be able to offer deep compassion, and unequivocal support, because you have been practicing being compassionate to the elderly woman at the park who wants to tell you about her bad knees. You have practiced by being supportive of a coworker when the copier is jammed minutes before their big presentation.

Your To Be List helps you to see opportunities to be the person you deeply want to be every day. It will actually help you enjoy making your way through your to-do list, because every item on your to-do list becomes an opportunity to deepen your experience of life. It will help you prepare to be truly present and aware so that when the grand opportunities of life *do* come along, you will see them, appreciate them, embrace them, and make the most of them.

And ultimately it will help you see that every opportunity that life offers you, whether large or small, *is* a grand opportunity.

Your To Be List is your way to a deeply fulfilling life. A life in which the mundane details of daily life radiate with the glow of life's luminous meaning. *Your To Be List* will help you stay connected to your soul's purpose, whether you are standing with your loved ones watching a tropical sunset, or standing in line with strangers to make a deposit at the bank.

The Miracle of Doing Many Small Things

Mother Teresa spent nearly half a century ministering to the poor, sick, orphaned, and dying in the slums of Calcutta, India. In 1979, she was awarded a Nobel Peace Prize for her selfless, courageous, and compassionate life's work.

She is famously noted for having said, "We can do no great things; only small things with great love."

At first glance, we may wonder if Mother Teresa's words aren't perhaps a little too modest. These were words spoken by a woman whose lifelong work of personal sacrifice to bring healing to the poorest of the poor in Calcutta made her one of the most beloved and inspiring figures in the modern era. If we were to ask a random passerby what modern-day spiritual luminaries they would most like to meet, chances are that Mother Teresa would turn up high on the list. Isn't that global recognition in itself the mark of a person who has done great things? And aren't Nobel Peace Prizes awarded to people who do great things for humanity?

But look closely at her words. Mother Teresa was not saying that great things can't be accomplished. She was saying: *even the greatest of accomplishments are composed of innumerable, small acts of loving-kindness.*

Mother Teresa's life work—work that earned her the highest honor for peacemaking the world has to offer—was not a solid block of goodness manufactured all at once. On the contrary, her work was artfully composed of hundreds of thousands of gentle touches, kind words, loving glances, courageous steps, compassionate smiles, creative thoughts, and inspiring visions. Mother Teresa chose again and again, each and every day, to be kind, loving, courageous, compassionate, creative, and inspiring. If you take away these "small things," the great accomplishments disappear with them. All great accomplishments are composed of small, yet meaningful actions. And all well-lived lives are composed of these deeply felt, well-lived moments.

Very few of us will ever become Nobel Peace Laureates. But, like Mother Teresa, we are capable of living lives in which the peace and happiness of others follow in our wake. We do this by making small choices to be the kind of person we want to be throughout the day. We must be diligent in our choices—faithfully, consistently, and powerfully choosing who we will be.

But first we must see that the choice is ours to make. Mother Teresa could have looked at the magnitude of the suffering surrounding her and fallen into despair, but she did not. She chose *To Be* Hopeful. She could have looked at the roots of poverty and become cynical, but she did not. She chose *To Be* Open-hearted. She could have looked at the daunting challenges she faced each day and been consumed by worry, but she was not. She chose *To Be* Courageous. She could have easily become bitter and hateful towards the people who turned away from the poor in disgust, but she did not. She chose *To Be* Loving and Peaceful.

The negative modes of being—cynicism, despair, worry, and bitterness—can sometimes become our default points of view. We might mistake them for emotions, but in truth, these are simply habitual ways of looking at the world. We fall back on them when we are feeling stressed, upset, and overwhelmed by the genuine emotions of sadness, anger, or fear. It is natural to react to difficult situations in life with these genuine emotions. We would not be human if we did not feel them.

But let's make no mistake; choosing to stay in default mode *is* a choice, even if it is an unconscious choice. The good news is that we have other choices, too: conscious choices. And these conscious choices are our "To Be's." At any moment we can choose to dwell in cynicism or choose *To Be* Open-hearted. We can choose to sink into despair or choose *To Be* Hopeful. We can choose to revel in anger or choose *To Be* Peaceful. We can choose to live in fear or choose *To Be* Courageous. We can choose to fester in hatred or choose *To Be* Loving.

We mustn't ignore our true emotions, no matter how unpleasant they might be. Instead, we must learn to take care of them. Imagine that your emotions of fear, sadness, and anger are a child who is hurt and crying. The child is calling for your attention, asking for your help. You wouldn't want to ignore her, or push her away, saying cynically, "Pain is what life's about, get used to it." That would simply be adding further hurt. We all know intuitively that the right way to respond to her would be to reach out with compassion and healing. You can do the same for yourself, when you have difficult emotions. You can choose to care for your unpleasant emotions with your "To Be's": be loving, be strong, be courageous, be balanced, be healing.

We are all human. We all struggle with negativity, even the most emotionally and spiritually developed among us. If you imagine that Mother Teresa did not struggle with these negative default modes, just as you do, then you are overlooking her remarkable strength and resourcefulness.

If you imagine that you cannot make the small but conscious choices that Mother Teresa made, you are overlooking *your own* remarkable strength and resourcefulness.

You may not be Mother Teresa, but you can make these exact same conscious choices she did each and every day by using *Your To Be List*. You were created with the same potential for strength and resourcefulness as Mother Teresa. You, too, can change your life, change your world, one "To Be" at a time.

Our To Be's connect us to the deeper meaning in life. And as Mother Teresa's life shows us, the small things we do every day, when infused with the meaning of our To Be's, become something much larger than they appear on the surface.

The more we engage with our To Be's, the more meaning gains momentum in our lives. Each small act that we fill with the meaning of our To Be's becomes like a small light that illuminates our path in life. The more small acts we fill with the light of our To Be's, the brighter and clearer grows our path toward meaningful living.

Mother Teresa's small acts led her down the path of infinite blessing and lit the way for thousands. It may be hard to imagine how choosing To Be Kind to the checkout clerk or choosing To Be Grateful for running water in your house or choosing To Be Patient when your child drops a plateful of rice on the kitchen floor may help you see your way to a richer, more meaningful life. But the truth is, once you shine the light of meaning upon your life, you will see that same light shining back at you from within every object you touch, every situation you encounter, and through the eyes of every person you meet.

In the next section of this book, Lauren tells the story of how a simple, wistful conversation that the two of us had when we were newlyweds, and a chance encounter with a newspaper article, led us to adopt two orphaned children in the midst of a war. Without the light of our To Be's, that conversation might have drifted into small talk and petty complaints, the article might have (literally) found its way to the trash heap and our two sons might be living their lives without the love of family. To Be's have power to transform our own lives and the lives of those around us.

Sorting Through Your To Do's

Aligning your to-do's with your To Be's is just a simple matter of sorting.

Throughout our lives we've had lots of practice sorting. When we were children we sorted things like baseball cards, Legos, dolls, action figures, rocks, coins, or shells.

Now that we're adults, our sorting tasks may not be as joyful as when we were young, but they certainly are necessary. We sort our laundry into baskets. We sort paperwork into files. We sort bills into piles. And we sort recycling into bins.

Now it's time to do a little joyful sorting again, like when we were children. The exercise below asks you to sort your to-do's into "To Be Bins". You'll have one bin for each of your To Be's: a Be Happy Bin, a Be Relaxed Bin, a Be Balanced Bin, and so on.

Sorting your to do's is as easy as sorting the recycling.

You just do the exact same thing with your to-do's. Simply look at the activity that's on your to-do list and decide which To Be Bin to put it in. Guide your sorting with this question: "Which To Be do I want to practice with this to-do?"

With recycling, plastic goes in the plastics bin and paper goes into the paper bin. With To Be Bins, you can be much more creative. Any to-do can go into any To Be Bin you like. In fact, you can put your to-do's into more than one bin at a time. You're free to choose where your to-do's go. That's even easier than recycling!

Let's look at an example. Let's say you promised to help your friend paint her kitchen on the weekend. She's just moved into a new house and she is excited about sprucing it up. She would love to hire a painter, but after the move, it's just not in the budget. Now it's Saturday morning. You made your promise to her on Tuesday, but now that it's the weekend, you really wish you'd never agreed to it. You're tired from the workweek and you really wished you'd left your day open. Before you call your friend and back out, try putting that to-do in a To Be Bin.

You have five To Be Bins in front of you representing the five To Be's you want to practice. Imagine your five To Be Bins are: Be Happy, Be Strong, Be Supportive, Be Loving, and Be Relaxed.

Where are you going to put that to-do?

Does it go into:

Be Happy?

Well, at the moment, you may not feel very happy. But you can choose Be Happy that you have a friend who depends on you. You can choose to Be

Happy that you're able-bodied. You can choose to Be Happy that you get to spend time with a friend on a Saturday morning. But perhaps you're really tired and grouchy, and "Be Happy" just doesn't feel right at the moment. So, let's keep moving down the line of To Be Bins.

Be Strong?

It takes strength to see through a commitment. Especially when you don't feel up to the challenge.

Be Supportive?

Yes. You are definitely being supportive by lending a hand.

Be Loving?

You do love your friend. And helping *is* a loving action.

Be Relaxed?

Okay, maybe right now that feels like a stretch. But it's possible that once you get into the flow of the day, and the right frame of mind, it could be relaxing just to hang out and talk while you're painting.

So there you go. By helping your friend paint, you can choose to be strong, supportive, and loving.

If "strong, supportive, and loving" is the kind of person you want to be, if that's what you'd like people to say about you when you're not there, then painting with your friend turns out to be the perfect opportunity to practice being that person. And you may even find that you can be happy and relaxed in the process.

It's In a Bin or It's In the Trash

Sorting your daily to-do's into *Your To Be List* is also a great way to keep you on track. *Your To Be List* helps you make sure the activities that you are actually doing on a day-to-day basis are the activities that serve your greater purpose.

When you sort your bottles, cans and newspaper into recycling bins, you are pledging to renew the materials, rather than simply consuming them.

When you sort your chores, errands, and obligations into To Be Bins, you are pledging to renew the energy you spend on the activities, rather than simply consuming the energy. If your to-do's consume your energy all day, you're exhausted and overwhelmed by dinnertime. If you recycle all that energy into To Be's, you breathe joy and peace into your day.

So, for example, if you were to schedule a conference with your child's teacher about some trouble they were having in math, and in doing so you chose To Be Strong and Compassionate, then you are renewing your energy: You are putting mental and emotional energy into the task and you are getting strength and compassion out. When you are able to take a to-do and put it on *Your To Be List*, you automatically know that it is the right thing to do.

Then there are the things that crop up in your life that are not on your to-do list, but which you can easily see finding your way onto *Your To Be List*. Let's say a colleague comes to your desk and asks for your help to resolve a conflict they are having. It's not on your list of things to do that day, but on the other hand, you can see that this is important. You choose to spend some time helping them, and in so doing, practice being helpful, honest, and understanding. This is a case where the task was clearly on *Your To Be List*, and just needed to be added to your to-do list. It's worth spending your time and energy if your energy can be renewed.

And of course there will be those to-do's that, no matter how hard you try, you cannot find a To Be Bin to put it in. You can't find a reason to Be Happy about it. You can't Be Grateful. It's going to deplete your strength.

Let's say, for example, you are invited to go out to dinner with some acquaintances who you know are usually negative or closed-minded. You have been out with this group of people before and you have always walked away feeling downhearted and drained. Well, it's no wonder. You are put-ting energy into this to-do and you are getting nothing out. That's energy that's being consumed, not renewed.

In cases like these—where a to-do does not make sense in *Your To Be List* no matter how creatively you try to make it fit—consider crossing that to-do off your list altogether. Why are you are hanging on to it? Does it re-ally make sense for you?

Finally, there are those things that crop up that are on neither your to-do list nor *Your To Be List*. Idle gossip. Hostile interactions. Self abuse. These are the things that diminish you in every way. They consume your precious time and energy, and they make you feel smaller and weaker. These definitely belong in the trash. Take them out to the curb and leave them there. They have no place in your inner sanctum.

Whether a To Be winds up in a bin or in the trash is your choice. You will intuitively know when you are making the right choice, because when you do, you will feel your inner light shining. And you will see it reflected in the world around you.

How To Make Your To Be List

Now that you understand how to use your To Be Bins, making your actual To Be List is a snap.

Let's say you picked the following To Be's for *Your To Be List*:

* *Be Patient*
* *Be Loving*
* *Be Courageous*
* *Be Open-minded*
* *Be Grateful*

And here is your list of to-do's:

- *Organize shelves in garage*
- *Call gas company re: overcharge*
- *Type up notes from committee meeting*
- *Take dog to vet for annual shots*
- *Find recipes for dinner party*
- *Balance checking account*
- *Take package to post office*

Some of the tasks on this to-do list are things you might look forward to doing. Some might feel boring, but relatively painless. Others might seem downright unpleasant. But if you get them all on *Your To Be List*, all of these tasks—whether they seem enjoyable or dull or anxiety-inducing—can become meaningful and affirming of your highest purpose.

So without further ado, let's get to sorting.

- *Organize shelves in garage*

   Organizing your shelves could take a while, and be rather tedious, so you can practice at Being Patient. If facing disorganization fills you with dread, you can practice Being Courageous. And in order to know what stays and what goes, you can practice Being Open-minded.

- *Call gas company re: overcharge*

   You definitely will need to choose to Be Patient as you are routed through the company's automated answering system. When you get on the line with that overworked, overstressed, underpaid customer service agent, you will not only get to practice being patient, you can also choose to Be Loving (yes, loving!). And in order to be loving, you will need to Be Open-minded: Imagine this person as your daughter, your aunt, or your best friend.

- *Type up notes from committee meeting*

   This is a great chance to practice Being Grateful. You have a computer to work on. And you can E-mail the notes out immediately. Enjoy the ease that this amazing technology affords you.

- *Take dog to vet for shots*

   Once again, you can choose to Be Grateful that your pet has access to such competent and compassionate healthcare (and don't forget to express your gratitude sincerely so you can watch the vet's face light up!). And you can Be Loving to your pet as your comfort him through his anxiety.

- *Find recipes for dinner party*

Be Open-minded! Be Courageous! Try something new! Be Loving! Think of your friends who will get to enjoy this food. Hold them in your heart as you plan. Be Grateful! What a grand opportunity to serve the people you love.

- *Balance checking account*

If you are one who tends to avoid your financials like the plague, this is a perfect time to practice Being Courageous. Face those numbers with a strong and brave heart. Be Grateful that you have the capacity to understand these numbers. Be Open-minded and try to allow the numbers to speak to you of abundance, not scarcity.

- *Take package to the post office*

Oh, the lines at the post office. They are unbearable, right? But wait. You have always wanted the chance to slow down and do nothing. Well, guess what? This is your perfect opportunity to do that. Be Patient (and, as an added bonus, this will help you Be Relaxed!) Be Open-minded: don't think of those people in line in front of you as obstacles on your path to the counter, think of them as real human beings, with real life stories, and reasons to talk to the postal clerk that are just as important as yours. Open your heart and Be Loving toward them for their humanity. And Be Grateful. Show your gratitude when you get to the front of the line. Do you know how many people get to the counter and glower at the clerk as if she is personally responsible for their anger and frustration? Is she staring at you as if you are personally the cause of *her* unhappiness? Be Courageous! Smile at her anyway! Imagine what a grateful word and a loving smile will do for her day as well as her perception of herself. You may see the effects immediately. You may not. But understand that you have planted a seed of happiness in her heart. Who knows how it may blossom?

So now it's time to put your to-do's into *Your To Be List.* It will look like this:

* Be Patient
  - Organize shelves in garage
  - Call gas company re: overcharge
  - Take package to the post office
* Be Loving
  - Call the gas company re: overcharge
  - Take dog to the vet for shots
  - Find recipes for dinner party
  - Take package to the post office
* Be Courageous
  - Organize shelves in garage
  - Find recipes for dinner party
  - Balance checking account
  - Take package to the post office
* Be Open-minded
  - Organize shelves in garage
  - Call the gas company re: overcharge
  - Find recipes for dinner party
  - Balance checking account
  - Take package to the post office
* Be Grateful
  - Type up notes for committee meeting
  - Find recipes for dinner party
  - Take dog to the vet for shots
  - Balance checking account
  - Take package to the post office

So there you have it. Seven tasks that run from enjoyable to bearable to thankless and they have yielded:

- Three opportunities to practice being patient
- Four opportunities to practice being loving
- Four opportunities to practice being courageous
- Five opportunities to practice being open-minded
- And five opportunities to practice being grateful

If you only had your to-do list, you might have spent all your time working your way down the list, checking off errands and tasks feeling stressed, overwhelmed, and put-upon. You'd end your day feeling exhausted and worried about what the next day will bring.

But when you put those same tasks and errands on *Your To Be List*, there were (at least!) twenty-one chances to practice at being the person you want to be. How different will you feel at the end of the day? All day, you've been patient, loving, courageous, open-minded, and grateful. Think about how will you feel at the end of the day that you spent living *Your To Be List*: Energized! Satisfied! Free! And when you wake up the next morning you will have a whole new day to practice at being the remarkable person you truly are.

What a way *To Be*!

Part Two: Our Story, Our To Be List

Choosing To Be Free—How We First Envisioned Our Family

The first time we discussed adoption was the summer we were married.

We were graduate students living in Boston and had planned on driving to Maine for a getaway weekend before the semester started. One last chance to enjoy our summer as newlyweds before our responsibilities took over. It was a humid, overcast Friday afternoon, and we decided to leave before rush hour to take advantage of the freedom of the open road. But despite our plans to beat the traffic, we found ourselves lodged in the middle of it. A sea of tail lights stretched out in front of us. Apparently, thousands of other Bostonians had also decided to leave the city early—and we were inching along behind them. Storm clouds started gathering above us. When the rain began falling, the mood in the car became dampened as well.

We were silent for a long time, feeling hemmed in not only by the traffic, but also by our frustration and disappointment, which had become so palpable that they felt like additional passengers that had squeezed into the front seat with us.

I stretched my feet onto the dashboard to overcome my growing claustrophobia. I closed my eyes and listened to the sound of rain falling on the roof of the car. I began to relax as I listened to the windshield wipers slapping out a soothing rhythm.

Suddenly, I realized where I was really sitting. I was not sitting trapped in traffic in a rainstorm surrounded by thousands of honking, unfriendly strangers; I was sitting next to the man I had just married. In a private space. Just the two of us. Alone in a romantic summer rain, with hours to sit and enjoy one another's company.

I opened my eyes and looked at James and smiled. I reached out and touched his arm, and he smiled back. We were no longer trapped. We were free. Free to enjoy one another's company. Free to open our hearts and explore the future that stretched in front of us like an open road.

We began to talk.

We talked about our careers. What we wanted to make of our lives together. The cities we'd like to visit together some day. The adventures we'd like to take together. And the most exciting of these adventures would be creating a family of our own.

We loved the idea of having a biological child and looked forward to experiencing the miracle of pregnancy and birth. But we also knew that there were many children in the world who needed the love of a family and were denied it. It turned out that both of us had always wanted to adopt. We agreed: two children. One we would give birth to; the other we would adopt.

And then we smiled, feeling once again that we were joined by other passengers in our cramped little car. But this time, it was not the oppressive feelings of frustration and disappointment that sat with us. It was the spirit of the children that would someday become a part of our family. We could sense their joy, hear their laughter, and feel their love.

Eventually silence settled between us; a peaceful, joyful silence born of hope. The traffic began moving, reflecting the great sense of freedom we felt in that moment.

Not only were we on our way to our getaway weekend, we were moving forward into our future as parents.

Three years later we had our daughter, Mira. By that time we were living in Atlanta, where we began our lives together as a family of three. And in the midst of the joy of the pregnancy and the birth, and the miraculous stages of her growth that we were blessed to witness, we forgot about that conversation in the car. We forgot about adoption.

Until the day the doctor called with the test results.

Choosing To Be Happy—How We Found Joy In Difficult News

I was pregnant for a second time. For over three months I had carried the pregnancy, and I had all the signs. The swollen belly. The flushed glow. The nausea. The giddy expectation.

At twelve weeks, when I had made it through the first trimester, James and I shared with Mira that she would be a big sister. She was about as happy as a two-year-old could be. She kissed my belly and told her new sibling-to-be, "I love you, baby."

But at thirteen weeks, when James and I sat in the hushed examining room to listen to the baby's heartbeat for the first time, our doctor couldn't detect it. I held my breath and tried to listen for even the faintest sound. My eyes began darting frantically between James and the doctor. I could hear my own heart pounding in my ears. My eyes welled up and I looked plaintively to James for support. He reached out and squeezed my hand.

Seeing our anxiety, the doctor immediately tried to reassure us. It may be just too early in the pregnancy to hear a heartbeat, he told us. The pregnancy might not be as far along as we thought. We could come back in a couple of weeks and try again. Or if we'd like, we could have an ultrasound right now. A heartbeat could be seen before it could be heard—would we like to do that instead?

James and I looked at one another then nodded to the doctor. We were relieved. Of course it must be too early; that made absolute sense! But why wait and waste two weeks on worry? We'd just go ahead and do the ultrasound now. James pulled a Kleenex from the box on the examining room counter and I blotted my tears, smiled, and followed the doctor out of the room to meet the ultrasound technician.

In the dimmed room, the technician squeezed some gel onto my swollen belly and moved the ultrasound wand across it. I was familiar with the procedure, having gone through it when I was pregnant with Mira. It had been an easy, flawless pregnancy and delivery. And now as I lay there in the ultrasound room, I remembered when we had done Mira's ultrasound nearly three years before. Back then, the technician had to point out shapes that, upon close examination, were parts of her impossibly small body. Her elfin fingers and toes. The plump roundness of her tiny head. The graceful curve of her spine floating in that black screen, like a string of pearls lying on black velvet. I remembered thinking how much looking at that ultrasound was like examining a Picasso painting. How you had to turn your head and squint to make the shapes become body parts. How the beauty and delight of it required a trained eye.

Now, three years later, back in the darkened room, I squinted at the black screen and waited for the outline of that tiny fragile life to appear.

The technician was quiet, gazing intently at the screen as she moved the wand back and forth across my belly.

She stopped after a couple of minutes, replaced the wand and turned the screen away from us.

"I'll go get the doctor," she said.

Seconds later, the doctor entered the room and flipped on the light. He pulled up a chair and took my hand.

A blighted ovum. That's what he told us. An egg that had been fertilized, but never grew. It wasn't that the fetus didn't make it. There was never any fetus, he explained. Only placenta.

I tried protesting. The morning sickness, I reminded him. And I was already big enough to wear maternity clothing. And what about our daughter? We had already told her. She's so excited about being a big sister. How are we going to explain this to her? I broke down into body-racking sobs.

The doctor gave my hand a compassionate squeeze. "I'm really very sorry. I'll leave and let the two of you have some privacy."

The technician, who had stood by silently as we talked to the doctor, blinked away tears of her own, and on her way out she gently handed my husband a box of tissues.

James and I held each other and cried, mourning the loss of a child that would not make its way into the world.

In the months that followed we tried getting pregnant again with no luck. One home pregnancy test after another came back negative. More tears, now tears of frustration, were cried.

I went back to the doctor. I expected a pep talk or a pat of reassurance like: "This typically happens after a miscarriage." Instead, he looked at me with a gaze that tried to balance caution and hope, "I want to run some blood tests. Given your age (I was 34 at the time) I think it would be wise to see if perhaps you'll need support from a fertility specialist."

He called me when the test came back and said he wanted to run the test again—he didn't think the result could be right. When I asked him what he meant, he explained, "Well these results indicate that you have the fertility of a forty-five or fifty-year-old woman."

I asked if fertility treatment would be necessary.

"No," he said. "If this test is correct, then fertility treatment wouldn't make sense. The test indicates that you are no longer ovulating. That you have no more eggs to be fertilized."

My stunned silence on the other end of the line must have moved him to jump in with more hopeful thoughts, "But listen, like I said, I think there must have been a lab error. Premature menopause is pretty rare. And you just had a baby two and a half years ago, right? So let's not worry. Let's just do the test again next month and we'll take it from there. Okay?"

The following month I took the test again. My doctor called me at home to tell me the test results were the same.

This time his tone was not as lighthearted, but he assured me that hope was not lost. James and I could still get pregnant. I could go see a fertility specialist about in-vitro fertilization. James would be able to fertilize the egg. The egg itself, however, would have to come from a donor; another woman would have to provide the egg.

He paused, waiting for my answer.

Helen Keller once said, "When one door of happiness closes, another opens; but often we look so long at the closed door that we do not see the one which has been opened for us."

My doctor had just informed me that fertility was a door that was now closed to me. I could have chosen to stand defiantly at that door. I could have chosen to pound it with my fists and beg God for admittance. But in the breath of a quiet moment after the news was given to me, I heard the hinges of another, older door creak open. And from behind that door I heard the whispers of a conversation from years before. A young man and woman, just married, talked in hushed conspiratorial tones about their plans for their future.

"I've always wanted to adopt a child," says the young man, with a smile in his voice.

"So have I," answers the young woman, her own voice filled with love and wonder at his compassionate heart.

I gave that door from the past a gentle push and a brilliant light came pouring out.

I must have gasped.

"Lauren?" my doctor asked tentatively, "Do you want us to call the fertility specialist and make an appointment for you?"

I laughed. "No, thank you," I told him with bold certainty, "We're going to adopt."

And so in the wake of what should have been devastating news, a spark of a long-lost joy revealed itself to me. I embraced that spark and chose To Be Happy.

Freedom, Happiness, and a Small Miracle

We decided we would adopt from China. We knew that there were many infant girls who had been abandoned at birth and who were waiting for a loving family.

We did some research and chose the international adoption agency that we would work with.

We read Mira books about China. However, given our experience with the miscarriage, we chose not to share too much about the adoption with her just yet. We would wait until the time to adopt got closer.

James and I made an appointment with the social services agency that would do our home study. We drove to their offices, where we met our social worker and arranged for the dates that she would come to our home, meet our daughter and spend time with us to see how we interacted as a family.

We were on a roll. With our home study scheduled, we filled out all our paperwork. James was scheduled to leave town on a business trip, but we made sure that we had both signed the application to the adoption agency before he left so that the application could be filed as soon as possible.

Just before James left town, I began suffering with a mild stomach bug. I woke up feeling nauseated every morning. James asked if I was going to be all right, but I assured him it was not so terrible that I couldn't get through my day with our now three-year-old daughter. She and I would be just fine.

The day that James left, I dropped Mira off at preschool and decided to go to the gym and work out. I felt somewhat better; the nausea was still there, but I felt like I was on the mend. I decided I would feel much better after a little bit of exercise.

I was also in a buoyant mood, because I had an important errand to run: the adoption application was ready to go. When I was done with my workout I would swing by the post office and drop it in the mail.

As I drove to the post office in my gym sweats, I passed the grocery store and decided on a whim to buy one last pregnancy test. It might seem like an odd thing to do considering what I now understood about my fertility, but my thinking went something like this:

When I mail this application, we will embark on this remarkable journey of adoption. Our days of thinking about pregnancy are over. I am going to take one last pregnancy test to mark the end of the fertility journey and the beginning of our adoption journey. This time, the negative result will not be a cause for tears, but cause for celebration. It will be a symbol of my freedom from the past.

I took the pregnancy test to the restroom in the grocery store. My hands shook as I looked at the result.

Perhaps in choosing To Be Free from my attachment to having a second biological child, something in my body relaxed, and my internal chemistry was altered. Or perhaps choosing To Be Free is simply the soil in which miracles take root.

Nevertheless, I never mailed that adoption application.

And eight months later, our daughter Tamar was born.

Choosing To Be Peaceful—How We Released Regret and Guilt and Relaxed Into the Life We Had

It was now 2001. We were blessed. We had two daughters.

Mira was now four years old and her sister, Tamar was nearly one. Tamar was the light of Mira's life. Mira was so attentive to her sister's every need, we joked that Tamar had two mothers.

One unseasonably balmy winter day that year, James' dear friend from elementary school, Paul, came to visit us.

The three of us sat on our back yard patio drinking iced tea. James and I were drifting on the patio swing; Paul was rocking in a rocking chair. Mira was giving her baby sister gentle pushes on the swing. Tamar was squealing with laughter.

Paul shook his head in disbelief. "Is your life really as idyllic as it seems?"

Well, yes. We had to admit it. Despite moments of chaos that accompany life with two small children, life was pretty idyllic. And we were deeply grateful for it.

But every so often, we would drive down the road where the home study agency was—the place where we initiated the adoption process—and I would feel a pang of sadness for the child we were meant to adopt. I felt that by being given one gift, another had been withheld. In my mind's eye, I pictured a little girl in an orphanage in China waiting for parents who would never arrive. I looked out at the very full and wonderful life that I shared with my husband and our two daughters and it appeared to me that something—*someone*—was missing. Of course, I felt more than a little guilty about having these feelings at all. Here we were, blessed with the birth of a child who we were told we could never have. She was beautiful and sweet, bright and healthy—and we loved her to the stars and back. It was not that I felt ungrateful for the miraculous turn of events. Far from it. Every day I stood in wonder at the gift we had been given.

But somehow I felt that, while we were on the road to adoption, we suddenly stumbled onto a detour. And it turned out that the detour—the road that led to the birth of our second daughter—was beautiful beyond compare. Stunningly, breathtakingly beautiful. Yet, there was a path that we had long dreamed of traveling, and we had only begun to walk that path when we had to turn and walk the other way. And then there was worry that there may be a child at the end of that path waiting for parents who might never come. That thought made me feel a deep sense of sadness that made no sense in the context of the joyful life I had been gifted. In the midst of my sadness, I wondered how I could possibly be so ungrateful.

For a long while, I kept my feelings to myself. I made a quiet home in my guilt and took up residence there. Alone.

The loneliness of my feelings pained me. I felt isolated from my family and there was a pronounced dissonance between the feelings of togetherness that my family inspired in me and the profound loneliness I felt as I isolated my feelings from the people I loved most.

One evening I finally chose to share my feelings of regret with James. I realized that I should trust in his love and his understanding. I should stop wrestling my feelings alone; I should open the doors to my heart and air out its dark corners. I told him about the pangs I felt as I passed the home study agency. I told him about the image of the child who was still waiting for us. I told him that I felt like the world's biggest ingrate. How could I be grieving for a child I'd never held when I could reach out and touch miracles in my own living room?

My husband held my hand and told me he understood. He shared my thoughts. He shared my feelings. I was never as alone as I imagined. The discord I was feeling was a product of illusions of separation and isolation. And it was these illusions that had imprisoned me. Releasing my guilt and loneliness allowed me to flow once again in harmony with my life. A deep sense of peace washed over me and I saw the light shining once again within my life. And what's more, I saw that the little girl in China would find another family: the family that was meant to be hers all along.

I chose To Be Peaceful and when I did, I saw the true blessing of our family. We had love and understanding. Love was where James and I began our journey together as a family. Love was where we stood. And no matter where the road of life would lead us, love would be our family's destination. We were never off the path we were meant to be on. We were standing precisely where we needed to be.

Choosing To Be Loving—How our Hearts Reached Around the Globe and Connected with a Little Boy Half a World Away.

One day that Spring, while Mira was at preschool and Tamar was napping, I sat reading the newspaper and came across an article with a photograph that caught my eye and tugged at my heartstrings.

The photograph showed a mother and a father, both white, with their daughter, who appeared to be Asian. The headline indicated that story was about the family's adoption.

Just as I was about the read the article, Tamar woke from her nap and cried out for me. I tossed the newspaper onto the kitchen counter and went to pick up my daughter from her crib. I left the article, unread, where it lay.

For several days afterwards, every time I saw that newspaper, I would think to myself, "I need to read that article." But life has its demands and distractions. It seemed like each time I intended to read the article, the phone would ring or the baby would cry or Mira would need help dressing her Barbie doll. I never got to read the article—and eventually that newspaper got buried under a stack of other newspapers. Then the pile of newspapers, with the article buried somewhere in the middle, found its way into the recycle bin.

And then I forgot about it.

Until one afternoon, as I was standing at the kitchen sink loading dishes in the dishwasher, gazing absentmindedly out the window at the trees drifting in the spring breeze, I heard the recycling truck rumbling up the street.

The article! The picture of the little girl smiling in her parents' warm embrace flashed in my mind. I dashed out to the street as fast as my legs could carry me and began rummaging though the recycling bin. I found the article just as the truck pulled up to our curb. I yanked it out of the bin and held it aloft in victory. As the recycling collectors waited for me to step aside, I waved my arm in a welcome gesture letting them know that they were free to take the rest. I had rescued my treasure.

I tucked the newspaper under my arm, went back into the house, brewed myself a cup of tea, and sat down to read the article. It was written by a woman who had recently returned from a trip to Kazakhstan, where she and her husband had adopted their four-year-old daughter, a little girl named Biba. The mother told of her profound love for her daughter, and how the experience had changed not only her daughter's life, but her life and her husband's.

The article ended with a plea to potential adoptive parents:

"Our daughter, Biba is now part of our family, but our hearts continue to grieve for all the other boys and girls who are still waiting for a family. Can you go for them?"

My heart leaped. Yes, it answered. Yes, we can.

When James got home from work that night I showed him the article. "I think it's time," I told him.

He looked up from the article. "Yes," he replied, "It's time."

And so we began to do some research. We found an adoption agency that specialized in adoptions from Kazakhstan. We called them and told them we were interested in adopting a girl. The agency's director was very kind and approachable. We told her about our history, about our plans to adopt a little girl from China. About the article in the paper about the little girl from Kazakhstan. She listened intently and compassionately, then asked if we had ever considered adopting a boy. No, we told her, we hadn't. Boys are harder to place, she told us. Would we consider adopting a boy?

In fact, the thought hadn't occurred to us. But we said we would think about it. We would talk about it. We would open our hearts to that possibility.

That evening after the girls had gone to bed, James and I sat down together to look at the agency website. There were pictures of many beautiful children. First we looked at the girls. All of them were beautiful. We smiled at each face. We pointed out each delightful feature, each charming turn of the head or glint of the eye. Then we looked at the boys. Again, we were so moved as we looked at the faces of these beautiful children, each child waiting for someone to call their "forever family."

We came across the picture of a little baby boy wearing a green outfit and, underneath the photo, was the name "Askar K." He wore a sort of stunned, innocent look on his perfectly round face. His head was covered with a hint of downy, black hair. "Look how cute this little boy is," I told James. Then I tried scrolling down—but the screen was frozen on his face. I couldn't scroll up or down.

I shrugged and rebooted the computer, and went back to the website. When I got to the picture of little Askar, the screen froze again.

Our computer had never done that before. I shut it down again, not consciously giving it a second thought.

The following day, Mira had a play date with a little friend of hers from ballet class. Her mom and I had become close friends, and that day she and I were sitting together watching the girls play in the back yard. I was talking to her about the unusual events that had happened in our family that week. I told her about the article in the paper. About my conversations with James. About the agency. About the pictures of the children we had seen. When I got to the part about the computer screen freezing on Askar K.'s picture, my friend took me by the hand and looked at me with twinkling, wise eyes.

"You know what that means, don't you?" she asked me, much in the same way as you would ask a child who ought to know the answer to "What is one plus one?"

I just stared back at her and shook my head, waiting to be enlightened.

"Lauren," she laughed, "That's your son."

I knew she was right.

When I told James that evening tears welled up in his eyes. "We have to go get our son," he said.

And so we began. We called the agency the following day. By the end of the week, we had signed a contract with the adoption agency. We printed out a picture of Askar K. and tacked it up to the refrigerator next to photographs of Mira and Tamar.

Three pictures. Three children. Our two daughters—and now, our son.

Our hearts reached half way around the world as we began falling in love with Askar K. Although we only knew him from a picture, his presence in our home was now as real and as palpable as any one of us.

The choice to Be Loving hardly felt like a choice at all. Our hearts were wide open, happy and free, and through our hearts, love flowed unobstructed, unhindered by biology, distance or circumstance. We did not create this love, nor were we in control of it. We simply chose to open our hearts and we received love's blessing.

Choosing To Be Strong—How We Stood Firm and Discovered Our Own Power

It turned out that the work of completing the adoption required a great deal more attention to detail than we had ever imagined. (It's not at all like the movies!) An adoptive parent does not simply state their loving intention to become a parent and wait for the child to be offered into their arms.

In fact, adoption is an exercise in organization and perseverance. There are phone calls to be made. Checklists by the dozens. Doctor's examinations. Affidavits to be signed. Birth certificates to be located. Documents to be notarized. Papers to be copied and filed and mailed.

All the same, it remained a joyful enterprise for us. With each item we checked off our to-do list, we were that much closer to bringing Askar K. home. When we signed the contract with our adoption agency it was May. We were told that if we could complete our paperwork without delay, we would most likely be able to travel before the end of the summer. We could be home with Askar before Mira started Kindergarten in September. Everything seemed to be falling into place just perfectly.

Then came the delays. We were told that delays weren't unusual, and nothing really to worry about. International adoptions required cooperation between multiple levels of government, both here at home and abroad. There might be delays caused by issues as serious as U.S. Immigration re-examining their policies regarding international adoptions, or by reasons as benign as local officials in Kazakhstan going on their family vacations. The delays in our adoption process fell more to the benign side of the scale, but were disappointing just the same. It looked like our goal of being home to hold Mira's hand as she walked into her first day in Kindergarten might be fading.

We asked if it was possible to hold off on our travel until after the school year had started. No, our agency told us. They had no control over when travel dates were given. What's more, it was typical that families found out travel dates just a couple of weeks before they were set to travel. Unfortunately, the government of Kazakhstan was unlikely to care about our daughter starting Kindergarten—and our desire to delay the adoption of our waiting child for the benefit of our biological child might send the wrong signal. They said that they were sorry that we were in this position, but there was really nothing they could do.

So we waited. And waited. There were days that felt like torment. We looked at the picture on the refrigerator door of five-month-old Askar in his little green bib overalls. But we knew that in Kazakhstan he was growing each day. He would celebrate his first birthday without us. We would miss his first words. We would not be there the first time he stood on his own. We would gaze at his picture and wonder what he was doing that day; what he smiled at; what made him giggle; what made him cry—and who would reach out to comfort him?

But as we waited, we were not alone. We were part of a group of parents who corresponded through an online support group. This group was comprised of parents in various stages of adoption from Kazakhstan: Some of us were waiting to travel, some were in Kazakhstan meeting their children for the first time, some had recently returned from their trips, and some were home and experiencing the ongoing joys and challenges of parenthood.

From time to time, the director of the agency would write with an important notice or a special request: One of the "baby houses" (this is what they called the orphanages where children lived from the time they were born until they were about four years old) needs more blankets, while another needs more clothing. One baby house needs more art supplies and books, while another needs monetary donations for plumbing repairs.

One day in early August, the director posted this open letter:

My burden comes today from the fact that some of the older children in the baby house are about to be transferred to an orphanage for older children. You see, they have turned four and the baby house needs to make room for more children, so these children are going to be removed from the only home they have ever known. They are going to leave the comfort and security and bonding they had developed.

It reminds me of the story that one of our families told me about while they were in Kazakhstan visiting their children. The said he was there one day when it was a day to "move" some children out and he saw a bus and heard screams and cries of the children, and he didn't know what it was. He asked the translator what was going on and she told him those children were being transferred to the orphanage. He said it was heart wrenching to hear them...

These four-year-old children are old enough to understand rejection, old enough to understand where they are, old enough to understand that others might get adopted, but not them, old enough to understand something is just not right. They see parents come and choose other children, and they understand: "It isn't going to be me this time either." They are internalizing this information and it is changing who they are and who THEY CAN BE! They can't possibly know what they may not ever experience, which to me is even more tragic! They don't know what they are missing: love of parents, warm beds with lots of stuffed animals, warm baths, nutritious food, a back yard to play in, neighborhood kids to play with, pools to learn to swim in, stories at night, love ALL the time, someone there for them ALL the time, security and comfort.

Remember, this post may not be directed at you, but if you pass it on, you might change a heart and help one of these older children find a family.

James and I printed out the letter. And then we shed tears over it.

Here we were, genuinely worried about how our daughters would manage being away from us during a temporary separation during which they would be cared for by loving friends and family. Meanwhile, just outside the door where our little Askar played and slept, was a group of children who were about to be separated from everything they knew and be placed in an environment where they would have to learn to fend for themselves.

Just a few months ago, the letter would have caused us to sadly shake our heads at the plight of these unknown children. But these children were no longer unknown to us. They were a part of us. We could feel their hurt and their loneliness and their fear.

We wondered aloud: Was this post directed to us? Were we truly capable? Could we manage it financially? It would nearly double our adoption costs. We would have to purchase a van, because we couldn't fit two toddlers, a preschooler and a kindergartner into our current car. Did we have enough room in our house?

And there were other questions, too. Questions that carried even greater significance. Were we prepared to be parents of four children? Was it fair to our daughters to double the number of siblings in our family? Were we emotionally prepared to bring a child into our family who had lived nearly four years in an orphanage? Could we truly understand his hurts or his needs?

In the end, we had no answers but this one: Whatever the difficulty James and I might encounter by choosing to adopt a second, older child— whether those difficulties were financial, physical, emotional or spiritual—these difficulties were nothing compared to what those children would face if they were forced to leave the only caregivers and home they had ever known.

It was like diving into the middle of cold lake, without knowing the depth of the water or being able to see the shore. All we knew was that we were strong enough to swim the distance and these children didn't even know how.

We called our agency and told them we would like to adopt Alisher T., a little boy whose sad brown eyes called out to us, "Come get me. Hold me in your arms. Love me. Teach me to smile again."

And so we chose to Be Strong. Because a little boy who lived halfway around the world needed us to Be Strong so he could smile again.

Choosing To Be Balanced—How We Learned to Care for Four Children on Two Continents

The delay continued through the end of August. The school year began. We were there with Mira when she began Kindergarten, but it was a rocky start. She had tears in her eyes as she awaited the bus in the mornings and in the afternoon she would step off the bus with a soggy tissue in her hand, trying to hold back her sobs.

We supported her as best we could. We listened to her fears. We understood her anxiety. We held her when she was sad. We told her that it would all pass, and that we were proud of what a big girl she was. We tried to tease out the small success stories and helped her to focus on the positive. We celebrated new friendships she was making. We applauded her ability to talk to her teacher and let her needs be known.

But in the evening after the girls went to bed, we were racked with guilt and doubt. We were still awaiting our travel dates. What if Mira's anxiety about school had not passed before we had to travel overseas? How would she find the comfort and support she needed? Perhaps we should take her with us. Perhaps we should take both girls. Immunize them and bring them along.

How were we to balance the well-being of our two daughters with the well-being of our two sons?

In just a couple of weeks that question of how To Be Balanced would take on deeper meaning than we had ever imagined.

The morning of September 11 began with the typical joys and challenges. Mira was in her third week of school, and we were relieved that her jitters had settled and she now bounded out of bed to meet the day.

Unfortunately, Tamar was not in such good shape. She had been running a low-grade fever for the past few days. This morning, though, what had started out as sniffles became a deep, painful cough and her fever spiked.

Once Mira was on the bus and James had left for work, I took her to the doctor where she was given a prescription for antibiotics.

While waiting in line to fill the prescription at the pharmacy, an elderly gentleman approached me. "Did ya hear? A couple o' planes just crashed into them Twin Towers in New York." I shook my head and told him that I hadn't heard that. It wasn't that I didn't trust him. It just sounded a bit outlandish. Like a game of "telephone" that had gone awry. Perhaps he had heard from a friend, who had heard from another friend—and somewhere along the way, the news had become confused or exaggerated. I thanked him for letting me know, paid for Tamar's prescription, and dashed out to the car. I settled Tamar, still coughing and whimpering, into her car seat. Then I turned on the radio, where it quickly became obvious that there had been no confusion or exaggeration.

I raced home and turned on the television in time to see the first tower fall.

And as I sat there with the desperate and sickening knowledge that I had just witnessed thousands of lives end, I felt I was also witnessing the collapse of our dream of bringing our boys home.

I called James several times at work before I was able to get through. "Please come home," I pleaded. "We need to be together."

That evening the E-mail adoption group exploded with fear and speculation. All domestic and international flights had been halted. Perhaps adoptions would be brought to a halt as well. No one knew how officials in Kazakhstan might react to this new crisis that the United States had been plunged into.

After we put the girls to bed that night, James and I stood at the threshold of the room that we had decorated for Alisher and Askar. The bunk beds that just the day before had spoken of a joyful union and unbridled hope in the future were now grave reminders of distance, absence and uncertainty. In the days that followed, our glimpses into that room were like looking into a hospital room where a loved one lay on the brink between life and death.

We realized that we were standing between two equally painful possibilities. On the one hand, it was possible that adoptions would be put on hold indefinitely and this room would stand as a crippling reminder of our country's and our family's sudden loss. On the other hand, adoptions might continue as soon as planes took to the skies again and we would be faced with the choice of whether or not to leave our girls behind and fly into a region of the world where the threat of war was looming like a dark and dangerous storm cloud.

Exactly one week later, on September 18, we received an E-mail from our adoption agency notifying us that we had been granted our visas and that we would be traveling to Kazakhstan on October 8. We would be part of the first group of adoptive parents to travel after September 11, and our hearts were torn between two very different sets of emotions. On the one hand, we were relieved to know that in a matter of weeks we would finally meet our two sons. We would soon get to hold them and kiss their round cheeks. The boys in the photographs would become real to us. The antici-pation of those first moments—which now felt almost like a reunion with our long-lost children—was almost unbearable. On the other hand, there was fear. Plain and simple. We would be flying half way around the world into a political situation that was unknown and more than a little sinister.

Friends and relatives would now pull us aside and earnestly (and sometimes tearfully) plead with us not to go. Their compassion and con-cerns were genuine and heartfelt, and we could tell by the expressions on their faces that what they needed to say pained them deeply. Each one of them expressed something very similar. Each told us something like this: "You have two beautiful daughters and a beautiful life. I know you feel you love these boys. I don't think you should risk what you have to travel right now. Maybe this is not meant to be. The boys will find other parents. There will be other opportunities to adopt down the line. But maybe now is just not the time..."

We listened with open hearts and with the same earnest intent with which these concerns were expressed.

But, in the end, we decided that we would move forward, and we ex-plained our decision this way:

Imagine you had four children. Two of them were safe at home with you. They were kissed at bedtime every evening and fell asleep knowing that the world was safe and that in the morning they would wake with the sun streaming in their windows knowing that a warm, loving embrace was just steps away. And then you had two other children, who were stranded on the other side of the world, caught up in circumstances beyond their control. Two children whose nightmares could not be soothed by a parent's loving touch. Wouldn't you walk through fire to bring those children home to where they belonged?

Our friends understood where we stood and the balance that it took to stand in the dizzying gap between two very different worlds.

We chose To Be Balanced, because the well-being of our four children required us to maintain our equilibrium. We chose To Be Balanced, because we could not afford to stumble when so much was at stake.

Choosing To Be Courageous—How We Moved Forward Despite Fear

To say that we were unafraid would not only be an exaggeration, it would be dead wrong.

Of course we had fears. We had very real, very pronounced fears.

We feared that something would happen to our plane. We feared that something might happen while we were overseas and that we would be unable to return. We feared separation from our daughters. From our sons. From one another.

We had no idea what might happen. We understood that, statistically, there was very little chance that we would personally be endangered in any way. The odds were that it would be a perfectly safe journey. But no one was able to offer us assurance that our travels would be free of trouble. How could they? The situation was so new—the wounds of our nation's trauma so fresh. It wasn't that we feared Kazakhstan. In fact, the one assurance that we *were* offered was that the people of Kazakhstan felt a great compassion for our country's suffering. Our fear was not a fear of a specific people or a specific place: it was a fear of the unknown. And that kind of fear is the most pernicious and dogged fear there is.

That fear lived with us as the day we were set to travel drew closer. Fear took up residence in our home. It spoke to us in quiet moments. It whispered to us at night when we tucked our daughters into bed. "Are you really willing to sacrifice this? Are you sure that is the wise thing to do?"

We knew that we could not shun fear and make it go away, but we also knew that we could not allow fear to make our decisions for us. We could not let fear guide our thoughts or choose our actions.

We knew that we must choose To Be Courageous. Not only for the benefit of our two sons, but also for the benefit of our two daughters.

I remember a conversation that James and I had as we discussed the possible grim outcomes of our decision to travel. I told James that I would rather our daughters know that we would risk our own lives to save the lives of two orphaned boys, rather than play it safe—retreat into the idyllic world of our lives at the end of a quiet cul-de-sac—and let two lives languish in loneliness. What we did for our sons, we would do for our daughters and vice-versa. All parents know that they would walk through fire for their children. And this grim chapter in our country's history provided us a chance to do that.

By choosing To Be Courageous, we found that we were supported and upheld by the courage of every mother and every father in history that ever stood firm in order to protect the sacred ground where seeds of their children's future were planted.

Choosing To Be Grateful—How We Received the Gifts of Friendship
A few days after our decision to travel to Kazakhstan, there was a knock at our door.

It was our neighbor, Kimra, hand delivering a letter written by her husband, Spud:

Hello Neighbors:

Surely all of us, as Americans, have been touched, whether directly or indirectly, by the terrible and tragic events of the last week. I would like to take a moment of your time to relay how, in this particular instance, those events directly touch our neighborhood's extended family.

Lauren Rosenfeld and James McMahon with their daughters Mira and Tamar chose to expand their family by adopting two orphaned boys from the former Soviet republic of Kazakhstan. Kazakhstan is a large county north of Afghanistan. As I am sure you all are aware, Afghanistan is in the cross-hairs of the American retaliation efforts. Lauren and James are scheduled to visit Kazakhstan in October for a full month to get acquainted with their sons and then bring them home. We are going to have two more little boys in the neighborhood.

Unfortunately, Lauren and James have not been able to get any information as to the safety of their impending trip. I'm sure we can all sympathize with their reservations about making a trip to a troubled region of the world right now, especially as American citizens. Also, can you imagine the prospect of actually making the trip and then being unable to return to your daughters at home, because of fighting in the region?

Lauren and James have some pretty overwhelming decisions to make in the upcoming weeks, decisions that I, for one, do not envy. They are so in love with these children, that it is impossible for them to imagine living without them.

Kimra and I are asking for your support as neighbors of the McMahon family. Kimra had the wonderful idea of tying yellow ribbons around our mailboxes until our new neighbors come home. We wanted James and Lauren to know that our prayers are with them and that we support them. We know that God will provide them the strength and guidance that they are seeking. We just want them to know we are here for them.

Kimra has plenty of yellow ribbon available if you choose to participate. Please drop by during one of your walks or comings and goings to the grocery store. We are usually around. Kimra also has a bow-making device (damned infomercials!) that she is dying to use.

It has been amazing and wonderful to see our country come togeth-er. As Americans, we all get so involved in our own little worlds that we forget that we all have something in common. We are Americans and we live in the greatest country in the world. Unfortunately, some-times it takes a tragedy to make us remember that. This terrible crime against humanity touches all mankind, whether directly or indirectly. It now touches our neighborhood directly.

Thanks,
Kimra and Spud

The following day, as I drove out of our neighborhood to take Tamar to preschool, I had to stop the car as I burst into tears of gratitude. There was a ribbon on every mailbox of every home in our neighborhood. Both sides of the street were lined with yellow ribbons. For our sons. In expectation of our safe return and of their homecoming.

How could two children, unknown to all these people, inspire such a miraculous outpouring of love and support?

And the outpouring of support just kept coming.

Family members and friends reached out to ask how they could help us care for the girls in our absence. We decided that rather than cobble together volunteer opportunities, we would call a meeting of all those in-terested in helping us with Mira and Tamar while we were gone.

The evening of the meeting, our living room was filled with the lov-ing, kind faces of neighbors, friends and family members who would help us with the girls. Tamar's preschool teacher, Erika, would take care of the girls from evening until morning. My father would pick Mira up from the bus stop each afternoon. My brother Bill and his wife Debbie would spend every afternoon with Mira. Our neighbor Suellen would come over each evening and help Erika get the girls into bed. My friend Kim would make sure Mira made it to ballet lessons every week. Other neighbors would arrange plenty of play dates for the girls—and would make sure that they were dressed up and ready to go trick-or-treating on Halloween night.

We felt that we were witnesses to a remarkable emergence of spirit in the midst of an earth-shattering crisis. We saw in our neighbors, friends, and family what Martin Luther King Jr. called "beloved community". Dr. King often spoke of "the solidarity of the human family" and once stated that, "We are tied together in the single garment of destiny, caught in an inescapable network of mutuality." We saw in those moments, as our loved ones leapt at opportunities to help us unite our family, that these children, our daughters and our sons, were part of one larger, greater human family. That our destiny was their destiny as well.

We felt overwhelming gratitude to be embraced by the love, care and support of this beloved community.

We chose To Be Grateful in the midst of our community's and our family's love. We departed on the wings of gratitude, knowing that our daughters were loved and cared for by a family whose protective eyes and loving embrace would shelter them, and whose kind hearts would welcome our sons when they returned.

The two of us arrived in Kazakhstan safely, and with the awareness of the blessings of safety and those who provided it to us, our gratitude continued to flow. Halfway around the world, another family of friends—our Kazakhstani friends—reached out to us, guided us, spoke to us, listened to us, translated for us. They earnestly offered condolences for the losses that were suffered by Americans on September 11. They gave us food, shelter and reason to laugh and celebrate. We were so grateful to call our beloved community back in the States and let them know that we were okay. We were safe. We were cared for. We had found another beloved community half a world away.

Our hearts were brimming with love and gratitude the day our driver and translator took us to the orphanage. We were just steps away from the two boys whose pictures had gazed out at us from the refrigerator door every day for the past six months. (Before we left, our daughter Tamar would ask us to carry her over to the refrigerator every night and insist, "I kiss my buvvies [brothers] good night." We would take her in our arms, lift her up and she would plant a kiss on each of those two pictures). And now we would be able to kiss those cheeks ourselves.

And then the moment came: The exquisite moment when the boys' caregivers—the women who had lovingly cared for these beautiful boys since they were born—brought these two incredible children to us.

While we had come to feel that these boys were our sons, we were complete strangers to them. The boys were frightened of us. They squirmed in our arms and reached back to their caregivers for the safety and loving assurance that these remarkable women had always provided. All the same, we smiled. We knew we had a long way to go to earn their love and trust. But at the same time, we chose To Be Abundantly Grateful that the Divine One had provided us the opportunity and privilege to do just that. And there is no opportunity in the world more sacred—no privilege more profound—than earning the love and trust of a child.

Choosing To Be Bountiful—How Our Adoption Became a Gift to Others

Three and a half weeks later, the four of us flew into the Atlanta airport, where we first began our physical journey to Kazakhstan. But James and I were completing the circle of a larger journey: A journey that had begun with a simple, wistful conversation while sitting in rush hour traffic in Boston eight years before.

Our friend Kimra met us at the airport. After tearful embraces, we loaded our luggage into the car—and strapped our two boys (for the first time!) into their car seats. The boys sat there, watching this new world pass by just outside their car windows. They couldn't possibly understand the great gifts they were about to receive: the gifts of family, friendship, love and support. These were gifts that were offered to them abundantly and without condition.

As we drove by all the familiar landmarks that led us back to our home, we were overcome with reminders of the bountiful blessings that had led us on the road to our destination and which welcomed us home. We opened our hearts and let it all flow in: the blessings of home, family, love, kindness, support, understanding, compassion, joy.

Our hearts were filled to brimming with this remarkable bounty as we approached our neighborhood.

As we rounded the corner to our neighborhood, Kimra honked her horn—and then we saw a sight that will be etched in our memories forever: On all the mailboxes, where there had once hung yellow ribbons in hope of our safe return, there were now bunches of brightly colored balloons that celebrated the reunion of our family. And our neighbors stood by their mailboxes, smiling and waving to the two boys they had been waiting to welcome.

James and I burst into tears of joy and relief. And as we rounded the corner to our cul-de-sac, we saw a huge banner posted on our lawn that read: "Welcome home Alisher and Askar." And on that banner were pinned all the yellow ribbons that once adorned our neighbors' mailboxes. Standing next to the banner, laughing, jumping and waving, were our daughters, surrounded by the friends and family that had cared for them in our absence.

How can a single heart contain such bounty? The answer is it can't. Choosing To Be Bountiful is not a choice to produce bounty, but a choice to receive the flow of bounty. What we receive in bounty we cannot contain. Bounty flows into and through us. We receive it, but it is not ours to keep. It does not belong to us. It belongs to the world. We pass it along to the world and that bounty touches the lives of others in ways that we cannot predict.

Recently we had the joyful opportunity to sit down and talk to our friends Kimra and Spud about those dramatic days we shared together as we sought to bring our boys home. We shared with them how that bounty we had received had blessed our lives infinitely. And they revealed something quite remarkable to us:

They felt that it was *their* lives that had been blessed through our adoption. They felt their hearts were opened to an understanding of how love crosses great divides of space and time. They understood how all of us on this earth are linked together as one family; how the fate of each human being is linked to the fate of every other human being. (Here, we thought it was our bounty, but they thought it was their bounty!)

Their lives had been changed forever by this bounty that flowed through our community.

That bounty will continue being passed along to all those whose lives are touched by our friends Kimra and Spud. It will continue to be passed along—from person to person—from community to community.

By choosing To Be Bountiful, we allow the blessings of life to flow through us to touch and change the lives of others in ways we might never imagine.

Choosing To Be Healing—How the Mundane Became the Sacred

There were many places in the world that were torn asunder at that time. Places that can be identified on a globe and places that can only be found in the hidden recesses of the human heart. Two towers fell. Our country went to war. Two innocent children were separated from their biological mothers due to social and economic circumstances that were beyond their control. Hearts were broken. Lives were separated. Wounds were opened wide. There was loneliness. There was pain. There was suffering.

And in the midst of it all, there was healing. Strangers reached out to one another with hearts of compassion. Neighbors, family and friends reached out to help in any way they could. Borders were crossed. Understanding was opened. Bounty flowed. Two children found a family.

There is a teaching in the Jewish mystical tradition that explains that our world is broken; shattered into innumerable and potentially dangerous shards. When we fail to see the Divine origin of our world and each person in it as a sacred part of the Whole, we are bound to be wounded by the sharp edges of our misunderstanding. Yet there is hope in this vision as well. When we look with eyes of love and gratitude, if we seek peace and balance, if we act with strength and courage, if we open our hearts to the bounty of blessings this world has to offer and find reasons to be happy, then each part is returned to its space in the realm of the sacred. The light within each person is revealed. We become agents of healing in a broken world crying out to be healed.

We have been home for eight years now. And the light of the many healing choices that were made, by us and the many loving people that supported us, still shines through our family.

Most of our days are fairly mundane, which is in itself a kind of blessing. There is homework to be done, meetings to attend, carpools to be run, meals to be cooked. There are arguments to be settled, knees to be bandaged, tears to be dried and hands to be held.

Yet each of these mundane tasks offers us the opportunity to encounter, again and again, the sacred, meaningful dimension of our lives. And in each meaningful encounter is a decision To Be Healing. Which is precisely what each of us was created To Be.

Part Three:
How?

1

Be Free—The Power to Envision

We've all had the experience of being stuck. Stuck in traffic. Stuck in a long line. Stuck in a relationship. Stuck in a job. Or maybe just stuck in life.

But being stuck is an illusion. It is the illusion that we are out of options, out of choices, out of luck. Granted, it can be a very compelling illusion. When we feel stuck—whether we feel physically stuck in a particular place, emotionally stuck in a particularly entangled set of feelings, or spiritually stuck in the dark recesses of the soul—we have the sense that we have been cornered by life. We believe that we are bound to act a certain way, feel a certain way, think a certain way, or simply exist a certain way, because there is no other way to act, feel, think, or be.

Our first step in choosing To Be Free is releasing our attachment to the notion of "stuckness" and all the anger, frustration, bitterness, and sadness that comes with it.

A few years ago singer/songwriter Terri Clark recorded a song about the resistance to release anger. She tells the story of a woman who's had a fight with her husband. The song vaguely acknowledges (then quickly

> **RELATED TO BE'S**
>
> Be Empowered
>
> Be Light
>
> Be Open
>
> Be Limitless
>
> Be Playful
>
> Be Radiant
>
> Be Spirited

dismisses) that she has the choice To Be Loving and To Be Forgiving. Instead, she is, for now, choosing to be angry. After telling her husband that she simply is not ready to make up with him, she explains her resistance to reconciliation very pointedly:

I think I'm right; I think you're wrong.
I'll prob'ly give in before long.
Please don't make me smile.
I just want to be mad for a while.

Most of us can relate to that feeling. Somewhere in our consciousness, we are aware that there is a way out of that uncomfortable, stuck place. But rather than turning toward the light of meaning and connection, rather than choosing To Be Free, we choose to stay stuck, mired in the negative emotions that destroy our own sense of well being or even the well being of our relationships.

The irony is that we feel a certain power when we feel stuck. We can feel life humming within us at a furious pace when we are angry. We can feel very vital, and life appears especially vivid, when we feel righteously indignant.

Playing the victim makes for a good story. "I was stuck in line at the post office for half an hour," is a much more compelling conversation starter than "I went to mail a package and the clerk was so efficient and friendly." All of this—from the adrenaline rush of fury to the mirroring of our negative experience in conversations with friends and family—can feel like a powerful affirmation of our belief that life is out to get us. If everything that goes wrong in our world is truly personal, that means that the universe is conspiring to make us miserable; and if the whole universe is conspiring to make us miserable, then we must be at the center of the universe's action. That can be a strangely attractive place to be. Staying stuck can be very tempting choice.

In order To Be Free, we must first release the emotions we are hanging on to. We must let go of the compelling story of being stuck. And then we can turn toward the light of meaning and in the glow of that light, we will be able to envision all the possibilities in life that our personal freedom offers us.

When the two of us sat stuck in rush hour traffic in Boston all those years ago, it was natural to feel angry and frustrated. It was tempting to take it all personally (Didn't all those cars ahead of us know we had somewhere to go?!) But rather than choosing to feel trapped, we chose to use it as an opportunity to sketch out our future together. And out of that sketch came the image of adoption—an image that would ultimately change our lives and the lives of many others.

So the very first To Be on Your To Be List is the choice To Be Free. It is the choice to exercise self-determination moment by moment throughout your day. It is the choice to turn and orient yourself toward the light that shines within you, even if that light seems impossibly dim at the moment of choice. You can choose to be anything on Your To Be List, but first you must choose to choose: You must choose To Be Free.

The 10 How's

{ 1 } Wide Open Places—Be Free

In order To Be Free, you need the space to move around. You need physical space, mental space, emotional space, and spiritual space. When you feel cramped and crowded in your life, there's no way to feel free. But with so many things pressing on you, demanding your time and attention, how do you get out of the confinement?

The things that are cramping and crowding your life right now will always be there in some form, so the answer is not to get rid of them. The answer is to practice feeling the space within yourself—the space that's always there, even in your most overscheduled day.

Start with a nice big sigh: "Ahhhhh!" Feel your chest rising and falling as you breathe. On your next inhalation, hold your breath for a second at the top, then expand your ribcage to let a little more breath in, then let it go. Imagine your ribcage expanding out just a little more with each inhalation. Spread your arms out wide to the sides, and imagine your ribcage expanding to touch your fingers.

Feel it expanding from side to side and front to back. Breathe into that whole space and let it be easy and free. Take a few big, easy, free breaths like this, all the way out to your fingertips and down to your toes.

Now imagine expanding even more, beyond the boundaries of your body, and past all the walls that contain you. Imagine taking up your entire city, your whole state, out past the borders of your country into the whole world. Remember all the places you've been, and imagine extending yourself there now as you breathe in and out. In truth, you are there now—you have left behind cells, and memories, and choices—everywhere you've ever been. Feel yourself surrounded with space, extending across space, expanding into space, breathing into and out of the limitless space all around you.

You can carry this sense of spacious freedom with you into the rest of your day. What would happen if, the next time you started feeling constricted, instead of focusing on how impossibly crammed your schedule is, you decided to remember how spacious freedom feels? What if you could move through your day with a feeling of wide open, limitless space?

{ 2 } Put The Top Down—Be Free and Happy

Imagine you're in a convertible with the top down on a warm spring day. Feel how easy it is to enjoy all the sensations—the wind in your hair, the sun on your skin, the scenery rushing by. Your heart is light and bright, your cares are lifted, and being light is effortless. Your favorite song streams through the radio. The gift of music, wind, and sun come together to remind you of the freedom that resides within you.

Pretend you're in a convertible and enjoy all the sensations around you! If you can imagine it, you can embody it. The deep happiness and the freedom of the open road are available to you right in this moment. The sunlight of your mind, the wind of the spirit, and the music of the heart are yours. Smile and accept these gifts. They are have always been there for you. They will be there for you always.

{ 3 } The Puff in the Breeze—Be Free and Peaceful

When you turn yourself free from your cares and worries, from the earthly concerns that bind you into the minutia of your schedule, all of a sudden you notice the peace that was always there underneath. It's no coincidence: it's the mental chatter that masks the peace. When we let go of the chatter, we feel both free and peaceful.

Sit quietly for a moment and let go of your thoughts. Don't worry; whatever you were thinking about will still be there three minutes from now when you're done with the exercise. As your mind calms, imagine slowly morphing into a fluffy white dandelion seed puff. The quieter your mind becomes, the more you turn into the seed. When your mind is quiet enough and you have completed your transformation, a gentle breeze lifts you up into the air and carries you up with it.

You feel so free, just riding the breeze like a wave, dancing in the delicate air currents. Nowhere to be but where you are. Nowhere to go but where you're being carried. Nothing to do but what you're doing. No effort, no striving, no clinging. Just peaceful freedom.

When you're ready, lightly come back to the here and now, bringing your sense of peaceful freedom with you. Imagine what people will think when they see you floating through your day like a dandelion puff in the breeze!

{ 4 } Escaping Solitary Confinement—Be Free and Loving

Usually what's confining us is ourselves. It's our own limiting beliefs, our old "tapes" which play on an endless loop in our heads, our narrow views of reality, which keep us from feeling free. The best way to pop out of all of that is To Be Loving.

Being loving demands that we understand someone else, which immediately transports us out of our self-absorption. When we are loving, we see someone else's perspective, which broadens our own. A larger perspective gives us more space, more freedom.

Imagine you are at the grocery store, preoccupied with your thoughts, your projects, your worries, and you bump into an old acquaintance. Your habit would be to try to limit your interaction as much as possible so you can get back to your shopping, and your worries. But you remember Your To Be List, and decide that instead, you'll practice Be Free and Be Loving.

You let go of what you were thinking about and tune into how your friend is doing. You listen while they tell you about their recent victories and challenges. You empathize with them, giving them the gift of your heartfelt smile and your compassionate support. You nod your head, "Yes, I understand. I see how you feel." As you offer them your kindness, you can feel your heart becoming free, casting off the shackles of your own troubles, and reaching out to your friend's heart, with freedom and with love.

{ 5 } Single-tasking—Be Free and Strong

You've probably heard of multitasking, and may even be a master at it. Multitasking can feel exciting and exhilarating, but more often feels pressured, stressed, harried, and frenetic. It may seem productive, because you're touching so many to-do's in rapid succession. But multitasking is not the best way to practice being free or being strong. Multitasking is much more likely to lead to forgetting Your To Be List altogether, binding you to the minutia of your day instead of its meaning, and scattering your precious strength.

Instead, try your hand at "single-tasking." By doing one task with your whole concentration until it's done, you can actually improve your productivity. By focusing on one thing at a time, you strengthen your concentration. And you free your mind to concentrate on the meaning in the moment.

Imagine you're at work, on the phone with a customer. Out of the corner of your eye, you see an E-mail come in from another customer, requesting help. Normally, you would open and read this E-mail, perhaps even respond to it, while talking to your first customer. But today on Your To Be List, you have chosen to Be Free and Be Strong, and so instead you close your eyes and focus on the conversation.

Imagine tuning into the customer on the phone with all your mind and all your heart, so you're really listening to what they're trying to tell you. See yourself completely understanding their needs, both logically and intuitively, and responding perfectly, much to their delight. You complete the call with strength and freedom, pause for a moment, and smile with satisfaction. Now you calmly turn your attention to the next customer.

When you rehearse a single-tasking approach in your mind, you develop your ability to be strong and free when the time comes in real life.

{ 6 } Day Surfing—Be Free and Balanced

Imagine you're on a surfboard, about to catch a big wave. You get in the sweet spot, find your balance, and quickly stand up on your board and start surfing. What if you were to take a stance you thought would be perfectly balanced, and then stand rigidly, clinging to that posture, no matter what the wave and the board did beneath you? Wipe out—no fun!

Instead, we find our freedom by releasing our attachment to a static sense of balance and surfing the wave of dynamic balance. A dynamic balance is where there is constant adjustment, adaptation, and compensation. Static balance only works when the environment is stable, which, in life, it never is. Life is much more like a wave than a block of cement.

See yourself surfing through your day, making little adjustments here and there to react to the ever-changing wave of your life. See yourself completely soaked, going with the flow, and having fun. See yourself free from your rigid ideas of how your day was supposed to go, balancing from moment to moment.

Imagine that you're surfing through work and a colleague comes to you with a big issue—a real "showstopper." Instead of feeling unbalanced and burdened, you decide to try surfing this wave. You imagine seeing an enormous wave coming right at you. You point at it with exhilaration, and shout to your surf buddies. You all swim your boards toward it to catch it in just the right spot, then turn around and paddle like crazy to build up speed.

All of a sudden, you're in it, and you stand up, balancing perfectly, rocketing toward the beach, the sea breeze in your hair. You ride it all the way to the shore, coming to a gentle landing with a big grin on your face. "Let's do it again!" you shout, enjoying the breathtaking feelings of being free and balanced.

{ 7 } This Little Light of Mine—Be Free and Courageous

Perhaps you were taught this simple little song as a child. It's so easy to learn and sing that it's the perfect pick-me-up in your dark moments.

The song was written by Harry Dixon Loes in about 1920 and has been recorded by many artists since then. It has been known as a folk song, a civil rights anthem, a gospel/spiritual song, and a children's song. It's a simple and powerful way to spark the Courage within Freedom.

There are many lyrics, but try singing these:

This little light of mine, I'm gonna let it shine (x3)
Chorus: Let it shine, let it shine, let it shine
Everywhere I go, I'm gonna let it shine (x3)
Chorus
I'm not gonna make it shine, I'm just gonna let it shine (x3)
Chorus
Out in the dark, I'm gonna let it shine (x3)
Chorus

When we let our light shine, we are being free and courageous. We take our light everywhere we go (verse 2), and we easily and effortlessly allow it to be (verse 3). When we let our light shine, it dispels the darkness, like the flame of a single candle.

{ 8 } The Unfolding Sunset—Be Free and Grateful

To feel free, you must release the need to control everything. If you're trying to keep everyone and everything in control, doing your will, just as you want it to be, then you are not free at all. You have bound yourself to the people and things you're trying to control.

A wonderful way to loosen your controlling grip is to give thanks. For example, when it's your birthday and your friend is giving you a gift, you have absolutely no control over what's inside that wrapping paper. Your only choice is to be grateful or not. When you're being grateful, you're acknowledging that you are no longer in control, that something outside you is guiding your experience, and this is tremendously freeing.

Imagine that you are sitting on the porch of a cabin in the mountains, watching the sun set behind the hills. You feel so grateful for this moment of wonder, as if it was a gift, wrapped in glowing oranges and reds. Notice that you have no need to control the process—you are not trying to make it go faster or slower, or be more yellow or more purple. You are free from the desire to make it go exactly your way, and are instead in the simple state of gratitude.

What aspect of your life could you release by being grateful for its natural unfolding?

{ 9 } Un-limiting—Be Free and Bountiful

Limitation is the opposite of freedom. Limitation is also the opposite of bounty. What we all want is to feel unlimited—bountiful and free. But how do we shake ourselves free from our own limiting beliefs and behaviors? How do we un-limit ourselves?

Pick a limiting belief, or "excuse," such as "I'm too old to get what I want." First, crack it open by questioning it. Beliefs are not reality. They're just maps of reality. And like maps of old, they can be wrong. So say, "Even though I have this belief that I'm too old to get what I want, I realize that my belief may or may not be true. What if it wasn't true? What if the opposite was true?"

Next, displace your limiting belief by imagining its opposite. Imagine what your life would look and feel like if the opposite was true. In our example, you'd imagine that your age actually attracted what you want, that it turned out to be the key factor in bringing you what you want.

Every time you release a limiting belief, you improve your ability to be free and bountiful. Crack open your beliefs, one at a time, by questioning their validity. Then displace them by imagining the opposite.

{ 10 } The Sea Breeze—Be Free and Healing

The act of releasing is at once freeing and healing. If you want To Be Free, you can't hold onto your worries or troubles, or even your hopes and dreams. Anything you're holding onto will keep you right where you are. If you were trying to cross the street, but wouldn't let go of the traffic pole at the corner, you'd never be free to cross, even when you got the "Walk" signal.

The act of releasing creates healing because gripping sends the message to your body and mind that you are incomplete—that you need the thing you are holding onto in order to survive. When you're attached, your body and mind go into survival mode, which takes precedence (rightly so) over healing mode.

Releasing anything—your worries, doubts, fears, thoughts, feelings, loves, passions, hopes, dreams, illness, even good health—is healing and freeing. Don't worry that the good stuff won't come back, just as it always has and always will. When you let go, you open to the natural flow of life. Whatever is good for you will come back in bountiful supply.

Imagine you are on a sandy beach, walking along the shore. There's a stiff wind blowing off the ocean—cool, salty, fresh. Feel the wind tussling your hair, rippling your clothing, softening your skin.

Imagine the wind blowing through you. Let it penetrate every muscle fiber in your body, cleansing, purifying, releasing, making whole. Let your troubles be taken by the wind, blown away down the beach. Let go of your fears and watch them tumble away. Spread your arms wide, and let the wind take everything you have, filling you up with its freedom and healing.

2

Be Happy—The Power to Enjoy

Do you remember being a small child and waiting for your best friend to come over to play? You would sit on the front stoop of your home waiting for her to arrive. You would distractedly scratch the dirt with a stick. Grind rocks into the sidewalk with your toe. Every so often, you might look up the street to see if she had rounded the corner. You had a picture in your head of exactly what she would look like as she skipped toward you: the smile she would have on her face, the spring in her step, the song that would fill the air around her.

RELATED TO BE'S
Be Joyful
Be Blissful
Be Optimistic
Be Cheerful
Be Wise
Be Insightful
Be Inspired
Be Creative
Be Positive

If she didn't show up when you thought she should, you would begin to worry. You wondered if maybe your friend might never arrive. Your boredom turned into despair.

Perhaps your mother might come sit down with you and put a loving hand on your shoulder. She would offer you a snack or offer to play a game while you waited. "No," you'd answer. "I'll just wait."

She might then point out that the sun was shining, that the birds were singing. "It's a beautiful day, after all," she would say. But you could not see the sun shining or hear the birds singing because all you could see was the picture of your friend in your head. All you could hear was the sound of her voice echoing in your ears.

And so you would wait and wait, becoming more unhappy with each and every passing minute.

As adults, we have the same feeling about happiness. We have an idea in our head of just what happiness should look like. And we withhold our enjoyment of life until that happiness arrives.

But all the while, true happiness, like the mother in the story, is constantly offering us opportunities to feel joyful. We simply need to open our hearts to the nourishment, the delight, the beauty, and the music of life that is always available to us.

Happiness speaks to us all the time, but we're not always willing to listen to it. Like the child in the story, we distrust what is being offered to us. We are fixated on our own *idea* of happiness, so we turn our backs on the *reality* of happiness.

The child wonders: how can just a singing bird make me happy when what I really want is my friend to play with? An adult may wonder: How can just a friend make me happy when what I really want is a romantic relationship?

When we look out into the world and all we can see is that the world is withholding the key to our happiness, then we will be blinded to the infinite possibilities for happiness arrayed before us. When the two of us wanted to have a second biological child, we were so fixated on the goal of pregnancy, and so certain that a pregnancy was the key to our happiness, that we were unable to recall that adopting a child was what we had wanted for our family to begin with. When the possibility of pregnancy was withdrawn from us, we were able to see the dream of adoption shining once again. True happiness came when we released our *idea* of happiness.

When you choose To Be Happy, you are looking at the world with fresh eyes. You let go of your singular focus and allow the real beauty that surrounds you to flood your field of vision. You will see that the wonders of life are always with you, supporting you, and offering you infinite opportunities to feel connected to happiness.

The 10 How's

{ 1 } Lady Bird—Be Happy and Free

As First Lady, Lady Bird Johnson established a highway beautification program. The wildflowers that now grow by many U.S. highways are the legacy of her vision. Lady Bird knew that to be happy, we have to enjoy the beauty in every moment, even the moments spent on a freeway.

Where she saw gray faceless stretches of pavement, she envisioned gardens of color. She freed herself from the tyranny of the status quo and imagined a more beautiful way. You, too, can free yourself from the drabness of your to-do list and choose to plant beauty and meaning in every moment using Your To Be List.

Imagine that you are a magical Lady Bird, and that with every step you take, wildflowers spring up all around you. See the daffodils, zinnias, and bluebonnets sprouting as you walk, leaving a spectrum of petals in your wake. You are creating a trail of happiness for your fellow travelers.

Imagine that wherever you go, beauty and joy follow. People see you and smile. Everyone loves to be around you, because they know you bring color, freshness, and cheerfulness.

With every step, you reassert your freedom to choose beauty. With every step, you choose once again to be happy. Each moment is a moment of choice, and you choose anew each moment to transform dreary to delightful.

Wherever you are, plant wildflowers there.

{ 2 } Tour Guide—Be Happy

Sometimes it's easier to appreciate things from the outside. It's the "Grass is always greener on the other side of the fence" phenomenon. You're so deep inside the details of your life, so close to your problems and worries, that you forget to notice all the many things there are to be happy about. Sometimes you have to get an outside perspective to see what's so great about what you've got.

Imagine you are a tour guide, escorting a group on a sightseeing expedition around your life. A pack of tourists in comfortable shoes and splashy Hawaiian shirts are trailing behind you, their cameras poised and ready to shoot; they're eager to capture their memories on film. As you go, you point out the many reasons you have To Be Happy throughout the day, as if they were National Points of Interest.

You: If you'll follow me to the bathroom, you'll see that I have clean, running water. This enables me not only to take hot baths and showers, but also to get a healthy drink whenever I please.

Tourists: Ooohh... (Sounds of shutters clicking)

You: Now if you look just over my shoulder you will see a window with the sunlight shining through. If you turn slowly, you'll see that sunlight reflecting playfully all around the room.

Tourists: Aahhh... (More shutters)

You: Now, if you get very quiet, for just a moment, you will hear the sound of my children playing in the next room. They are all very healthy. You can hear that in their voices. At the moment, you will hear them laughing, as they are quite occupied with the games and toys that they have been given by loving relatives, of which we have many.

Tourist: (muttering to one another) Very nice. Very nice indeed.

Now admittedly it's silly. But you get the point: happiness glistens in everything in your life, just waiting for you to see it. You don't even need to leave the bathroom To Be Happy.

{ 3 } The Micro-Sabbath—Be Happy and Peaceful

The Sabbath is a whole day every week devoted to reconnecting with meaning in our lives. It's a day of rest from all the creating, the controlling, and the coping we do during the week. It's a day of peace and relaxation.

There's a delicious joy in releasing the week and embarking on twenty-four hours of time to just be. A day to watch the sun journey across the sky, to watch the grass grow and the leaves fall, to watch kids play in the fresh air. A day to enjoy being truly present wherever you are, fully awake and alive.

But you don't have to wait until the Sabbath to be peaceful and happy. You can do it any time you want. You can take micro-Sabbaths multiple times a day to rest and reconnect.

Imagine that you wake up feeling overwhelmed with everything you have to get done today. You have about three times as much to do as is possible, and just thinking about it, you're already feeling burdened and burned out. And you haven't yet even had your morning coffee!

As you step into the shower, you decide that instead of using these few minutes to mentally itemize the list of unrealistic demands on your schedule, you'll take a micro-Sabbath. You let the clutter wash out of your mind for just a moment and feel the warm water running over you. You smile as you inhale the steam deeply, enjoying the simple act of breathing. You serenely massage your scalp with shampoo. You soap up your limbs peacefully, quietly, happily. You smile at the towel as you dry off. Your micro-Sabbath feels so wonderful that you decide to put Be Happy and Be Peaceful at the top of Your To Be List for the rest of the day. No matter what you're doing, you're going to do it with peace and happiness.

You can take spontaneous micro-Sabbaths whenever you notice a spare moment in your schedule, and use them as little reminders to get back onto Your To Be List. You can take a micro-Sabbath when you first get into the car on your way to work, when you get up from your desk to get some coffee or water, when you go to the restroom, when you walk to a meeting, when you're just arriving home, when you're doing dishes, while you're brushing your teeth. Even while you're working your way through your unrealistic to-do list.

Micro-Sabbaths make your whole day much more peaceful and happy. They can be as long as a shower, or as short as one breath. When other people wonder how you got to be so peaceful and happy, tell them!

{ 4 } Happiness Drafting—Be Happy and Loving

You have the power to create happiness in other people. When you say a kind word, listen deeply, or offer your compassion, their happiness instantly blossoms. When you bring out the happiness in others, and connect with them, the happiness naturally flows back to you. You are swept along by their happiness, like geese flying in "V" formation to "draft" off each other as they migrate. The geese take turns being in the lead, creating air currents that make the flying easier for the whole flock. In this exercise, you'll practice helping someone else be a lead goose, then drafting off of her happiness.

Imagine you're having coffee with a friend who has been down in the dumps lately—she has seemed flat, uninspired, bored. You begin asking her positive-focused, open-ended questions, like, "What's been the most enjoyable part of your day today? What have you really loved doing lately? What's working well in your life these days? What are your big dreams for the future?"

You clear your mind and listen deeply to her answers, without preparing what you're going to say next. As your conversation progresses, you notice that she's becoming more animated and excited. By asking your genuine questions with a spirit of open-hearted inquiry, you're uncorking the sources of happiness that have been bottled within her and now are spreading over her like a fresh spring breeze.

Her face changes as she starts talking about what she really loves and about her big dreams. As you listen with your whole heart and soul, you feel the fresh breezes of her happiness tickling you, too. A smile comes to your face, and you're happiness drafting!

{ 5 } Comforting the Kindergartner—Be Happy and Strong

We have to stay strong to fully participate in the wonders of life. We have to be physically strong to enjoy a walk in nature. We have to be mentally strong to enjoy a stimulating conversation. We have to be emotionally strong to be able to enjoy a committed relationship. We have to be spiritually strong to enjoy the miracles of a steadfast faith.

Imagine that you are taking your five-year-old granddaughter to the park. You're smiling as you watch her playing with some of the neighborhood kids on the monkey bars. Suddenly, she runs to you in tears—one of the other children has hurt her feelings. You scoop her up in your arms and hold her tight, telling her it will all be okay. As you pat her head, you can feel her relax into the stability and comfort you're providing. After soaking up your stability for a few minutes, she wipes her tears, wriggles out of your arms, and runs back to the monkey bars.

In this tender moment, you are so happy for your strength. You are happy for your physical strength to be able to lift her up and hold her. You are happy for your mental strength to know just what to say to comfort her. You are happy for your emotional strength to stay calm and loving instead of getting angry with the child who hurt her. You are happy for your spiritual strength that helps you appreciate the meaning behind this moment.

Standing firm in the hardest moments takes strength, and provides access to the deepest joy life has to offer.

{ 6 } The Ski Slopes—Be Happy and Balanced

Balance requires intuitively adjusting to reality as it changes, while keeping focused on a steady point in the distance. Practicing being in this state of dynamic balance produces happiness in you. In order to adjust to changing reality, you have to be awake, aware and present to the world around you—this is a very happy state. And when you have your focus set on an unmoving point—your vision, your values, your mission—you ground yourself in meaning.

Imagine you're hopping off a ski lift at the top of a snow-covered slope that's just the right level for you. As you push off and begin the run, a broad smile jumps to your face. You savor all of the sensations of the moment: the crisp mountain air whooshing past you, the sunlight glittering off of the icy pine branches, the unmistakable sound of skis slicing through snow.

You settle down into a crouch and gather some speed. You are adjusting in real time to the demands of the slope—a bump here, a dip there, avoiding obstacles as they come. Suddenly you notice that your right ski is just about to encounter a six-inch snow-covered rock. Your body reacts perfectly, shifting your weight to the left, letting the right ski ride over the rock, and soon you are evenly balanced on both skis. You trusted your body's intuition and stayed focused, and successfully navigated a challenge to your balance.

But then you wipe out. An easy, gentle fall, but not so graceful. Skis crossed and covered with snow by the side of the slope, you're faced with a choice: do you get up cursing, or with a chuckle? You remember Your To Be List and that you had decided To Be Happy and Balanced, and you smile and wave as you stand up. That was just a bigger balance adjustment, you tell yourself. Then you're back on your skis, surfing the slope, intuitively adapting to all the little bumps that come your way, and staying focused on your goal: To Be Happy.

What if you could ski your way through a day of work? What if you could adapt to the ever-changing work landscape with as much agility as you had on the slopes?

What would it feel like if, when your kid spikes a fever and you realize all your plans for the next couple of days have just been rearranged, you could chuckle, stand back up, and keep skiing?

{ 7 } The Smile Wave—Be Happy and Courageous

Have you ever seen someone start "the wave" at a baseball stadium?

A solitary fan stands, raises their arms, and cheers. Maybe the wave never catches on, and the fan just sits back down sheepishly. But if that fan is a fanatic, the neighboring section will pick up on the enthusiasm and try to spread the wave even further. Within seconds, the stadium comes alive with the energy of that wave, and all the fun and excitement it carries.

What if that first fan had thought it was too much trouble, and had just given up? No wave, no excitement, no fun.

You can start a smile wave that works the same way. Make someone else smile as they walk down their own path, and you'll start a wave that will ripple out into the world in ways you'll never know.

Imagine that you're at the back of the line at the post office, and it's moving as slow as molasses. The woman at the front of the line finishes her postal business and turns to leave, but for some reason she looks over at you, and you notice that her face is full of concern. Her jaw is set, her brow is knit, and her eyes are troubled. Though your habit would be to ignore her and let her go about her business, you remember that Be Happy and Courageous are on Your To Be List, and decide to practice. You decide to put yourself out there and smile at her, even though it seems likely you won't get a smile in return.

You offer her your best smile: compassionate, genuine and from your heart. She clearly wasn't expecting a warm smile when she looked at you, and it catches her off guard. She slows almost to a stop, and her surprise changes to relief. As the corner of her lip curls up to reveal a sheepish grin, her face says back to you, "Oh, yeah, I forgot to smile! Boy, I sure was caught up in my worries there for a while. Thank you." In an instant, you wordlessly communicate volumes.

Eyes still locked, you take a deep breath and sigh while smiling, as if to say, "I know. It can be tough. Keep it up, and enjoy your day." She sighs back at you, and then, visibly relieved and reconnected with her own sense of meaning, she turns and walks out of the building.

You just started a smile wave. But where will it end? Perhaps she was about to get on a plane, and she'll take your smile to a distant land. Perhaps she was about to address an audience, and will pass your smile to everyone in the room. Perhaps she'll offer it to a young child. With your courage and happiness, you touched far more than the worried lady at the post office, but just how much more, you'll never know.

{ 8 } The Miracle of Broccoli—Be Happy and Grateful

Miracles are in the mundane. The extraordinary dwells within the ordinary. When held in just the right way, even the most routine details of our lives catch the light of meaning, and reveal the wonder just beneath the surface.

When you put Be Happy and Be Grateful on Your To Be List, you begin to hold things in just the right way, and you will start to see the miracles in the mundane.

Imagine you're standing in your kitchen, looking at something ordinary from your normal evening routine, like the broccoli you're going to try to get the kids to eat for dinner. Before chucking it into the microwave, you decide to practice being happy and grateful, and to look for the miracles inside the humble vegetable.

In an instant, a new world unfurls. Looking at the broccoli, you are grateful for the magic that allows tiny seed to know how to transfigure itself into a broccoli sprout. You are grateful for the life force that lets the sprout suck water out of the ground and pull nutrients from the soil. You are awestruck by the understanding that this little plant breathes life into the inert minerals, kissing them awake, transforming inert nitrogen, phosphorus, and carbon dioxide, into a living organism. You are deeply reverent for the sunshine that conveyed momentum to the gears of life inside the vegetable.

You enjoy the fact that you're not just looking at an individual plant, but a long and interconnected chain of life. The broccoli exists because of the farmers who prepared the earth, planted the seed, brought it fertilizer and gave it water. It exists because of the insects who pollinated it, and all the bacteria which fixed its nitrogen. It exists because of all of the previous generations of broccoli that descended through the ages to produce its seed.

You smile your gratitude to the tapestry of living beings that brought you this vegetable. You join your palms and give thanks for the blessed opportunity to witness the presence of these many miracles. You feel as if you are standing in holy sanctuary, because you are, even if it's disguised as your kitchen.

{ 9 } Treasure the Trash—Be Happy and Bountiful

Our minds are super–competent at classifying and filing our experiences. They do so quickly and efficiently, and enable us to survive in a sometimes-threatening environment. They allow us to process the millions of bits of information streaming at us all the time from our senses, and focus our attention on the most urgent stream. Unfortunately, our minds focus so quickly that sometimes we miss the bountiful treasure in what we're seeing.

Overlooking treasure is a trick of the adult mind. Children, on the other hand, are constantly finding treasures.

Imagine that your daughter has found a random piece of plastic on the ground and, with a wide and open grin, brings it to you to admire. "Look what I found!" she beams. Perhaps your first instinct is to tell her to throw it away. If it was on the ground, it's trash. Trash belongs in a trashcan and you certainly have better things to do than look at garbage.

But your daughter demands, "No, look!" She insists that you pay closer attention to her newfound treasure. And sure enough, when you look more deeply, you see what she sees—a rainbow emerging from the refractions of the sun's light. There, in that little piece of plastic, is a full spectrum of color, dancing and glowing.

You look up at her bright, shining face, and tell her, "Yes, I see it now—how beautiful!" As she skips off to find more treasure, you look around with fresh eyes. Everything seems to be sparkling. The tree leaves are twinkling like diamonds, the children's voices are golden, the air is lavishly overabundant, even the dirt seems richer than you remember.

A dented bottle cap catches your eye, and you lean over to pick it up. Your eyes grow wide, and you race over to your daughter, who is digging in the dirt with a stick. "Look what I found! See how it kind of looks like a heart? It reminds me of you!"

{ 10 } The Cellular Happy Dance—Be Happy and Healing

Our bodies are pretty smart, but they can't tell the difference between real and imaginary. When you go to see a horror movie, your body floods itself with the very same chemicals that it releases when you're really in danger. There isn't a "just kidding" version of adrenaline. And it has the same effect on the body regardless of whether the threat was real or imagined.

Happy chemicals are the same way—they don't care if you imagined them into being or not. So, why not go ahead and imagine them into being? Imagine happiness into being, and happy chemicals will become physically present in your body, healing as they go.

Imagine one of the cells on the tip of your right pinkie sitting around on its cellular couch, bored, watching the other cells go about their humdrum business. Suddenly, colorful swirling lights switch on, a disco ball drops down from the ceiling, and out of nowhere, a spicy dance tune begins to play.

Your pinkie cell leaps off the couch, straps on a party hat, and fires up a happy dance, like it just won the lottery. All the other cells passing by stop what they're doing, put flower leis around their necks, and join in. The party quickly spreads up your whole pinkie, to all the muscle cells, the bone cells, the nerve cells, the blood cells. Everyone wants to join the celebration.

Right now, wiggle your pinkie around, like it was dancing. Let your pinkie go a little nuts—let it boogie and shimmy to the imaginary music. (It's okay to smile at this—it's a little silly.)

Now, imagine the happy dance party spreading from cell to cell. Your whole hand is happy-dancing, then your wrist, your whole right arm, spreading across your chest, and all the way down the left arm. Soon, your whole body is wiggling and jiggling in a happy dance. All your cells are dancing, doing the bump, the cha-cha, the Macarena. They have lampshades on their heads now, and are waving their hands in the air with gleeful abandon. Wiggle your body around, feeling the joy flow through all your cells.

When you imagine your cells all happy and dancing, the electricity and the chemistry in your body change in very healing ways. Doing this exercise regularly will reprogram your biochemical computer. The more you imagine yourself being happy and healing, at a cellular level, the more this will become your natural way of being.

3

Be Peaceful—The Power to Relax

We all want to find the space and time to stretch out, to unwind, and to feel at ease in the world. But life doesn't always cooperate. There is just so much to do. We must go to work, cook, maintain our homes, and support the health and happiness of the people who live in them. We want to relax, but we wonder how we will ever find the time to do it. There is so much to do, and only so many hours in a day.

RELATED TO BE'S
Be Relaxed
Be Knowing
Be Understanding
Be Harmonious
Be Serene
Be Still
Be Calm
Be Accepting

Yet, when we look at the multitude of tasks that we need to get accomplished each and every day, we'll realize that most all of these tasks are aimed at helping us relax and enjoy life.

- We need to go to work to earn money to create a good life in which we can relax. And we may go to work to make the world a better place, so that we (and others) live in a safe, healthy world.
- We need to buy groceries so that we can fill our bellies, enjoy our meals, and relax.
- We need to keep our living spaces clean so that we can have un-cluttered and healthy rooms in which we can live and relax with our friends and family members.

• We keep up our yards and our gardens so we can have a beautiful space that we can sit and reflect and relax.

So relaxing seems to be a fundamental motive that drives much of our behavior. And therein lies a profound irony: *We are driven to relax.*

We want so badly to unwind, that we stress ourselves out trying to do it. And then when a moment finally arrives when we are free of deadlines and demands, we can't relax because we haven't practiced relaxation. Our inner drive is so strong and has gained so much momentum, that our bodies and our minds are humming with the energy of the drive to relax. In other words, we may be sitting on a beach towel looking out at the ocean waves, but we feel as if we are sitting on pins and needles and all we can think about is what we will need to do when we get home. Your outer landscape may be relaxing, but your inner landscape is a tangle of to-dos.

True relaxation does not mean the absence of tasks or responsibilities. True relaxation comes when we find peace in the moment, regardless of what is happening in that moment. So we need to practice relaxation while we are going about the tasks of our daily lives—and we do this by accepting the moment just as it is.

True relaxation comes with the choice To Be Peaceful: To embrace the moment and smile at it. We have the ability to feel relaxation wherever we are. We do not need to wait for coffee break, or a weekend, or a vacation. We do not need a perfectly clean house, a perfectly manicured lawn, or a perfectly serene forest glade. Relaxation can be found in the middle of a sales meeting. Relaxation can be found in the towels in your laundry basket.

Relaxation can even be found at a broken traffic signal that is stuck on red. We are always waiting for an opportunity to do nothing. Well, when you are stuck at a red light, you know what you can do? Exactly. Nothing. So breathe, relax, and enjoy your peaceful moment at the red light.

For the two of us, Being Peaceful meant relaxing into the life that we had with our two beautiful daughters. We had to accept where we were in our lives. It was impossible to relax into the reality of our lives when our minds were still attached to life-as-it-could-have-been. When we were able to release our ruminations about the past (and all the stress and remorse and guilt that came with them) we were able to be truly present in our lives. And peace was there, in that present moment, just waiting for us to let go of the past. Peace was there, ready to catch us. Ready to embrace us.

Peace is always there for you. When you choose To Be Peaceful you are choosing to relax into the present moment. And the present moment is the only moment from which you can move forward into a joyful future.

Relaxation can be found wherever you are when you choose To Be Peaceful.

The 10 How's

{ I } Turning to Sand—Be Peaceful and Free

The cause of all unease in your life is some form of attachment. When you're holding onto something—physical tension, a sense of entitlement, anger, even hopes for a specific goal—it causes discomfort. Whenever there's trouble in your life, ask, "What am I holding onto that's causing this?" Then make it your intention to let go. When you envision yourself without that tense attachment, you're practicing being free and being peaceful.

This exercise will help you practice letting go by imagining yourself slowly turning into warm, dry sand. Sand is incapable of holding tension—it is completely free to shift in perfect harmony with forces of nature.

Imagine your toes slowly turning into warm, dry sand. At first, the sand holds the shape of your toes, then gradually relaxes with gravity. Feel a sense of complete and total relaxation in your toes. Let your feet turn to sand, completely incapable of holding any tension. Let your ankles turn to sand, releasing all tension. Let the sand spread up your calves and shins to your knees, then into your quads and hamstrings. Feel your whole lower half as warm, dry sand, and let it relax with gravity, releasing its form, becoming a couple of dunes where your legs used to be.

Imagine your hips and lower abdomen turning into warm, dry sand. Holding no tension at all. Feel the sand spreading up into your stomach and torso, feel your whole backbone turning to sand. Feel your shoulders turning to sand, completely letting go. Let your arms and hands turn into sand, and then your neck and throat. Let your whole skull turn to sand, your face, your whole head just turning to warm, dry sand.

Throughout the day, you can practice turning little bits of you into sand. If your stomach gets tight in a meeting, turn it to sand, and for just a few moments, you can practice being peaceful and free.

{ 2 } The Smiling Raindrops—Be Peaceful and Happy

Peace and happiness are hidden in the simple things, the little things, the mundane things. Peace and happiness are like little diamonds concealed inside the seemingly ordinary rocks of our day-to-day activities. They're everywhere, inside everything, but they can only be found in the here and the now—and only if you intend to see them.

Imagine that you are planning a picnic, but just as you finish packing the cooler, you see that it has started raining. Gray rain clouds as far as you can see. After a few moments of feeling disappointed and cheated, you decide to get back on Your To Be List and look for the diamonds of peace and happiness.

You step outside to the front stoop and have a seat under the awning. It's really coming down now. The droplets closest to you splatter off the pavement and moisten your shins. You notice how soft and sweet the little splashes are. The air is fragrant with a muddy, earthy scent that brings back memories of being a kid.

As you relax into the moment, you realize that the sound of the rain is not just one monolithic voice, but is truly a chorus. The rain has one voice when it jumps on the roof, another when it plays in the tree leaves, and a third as it clatters against the sidewalk.

You look into the rain, and where before you only saw the grayness of disappointment, now you notice that each drop glistens. Each drop has a life of its own, and falls with perfect peace, perfect natural harmony. You smile at the drops as they serenely journey from cloud to puddle, and you have a sneaking suspicion they're smiling back at you. You and the rain enjoy a peaceful moment together.

{ 3 } The Still Pond—Be Peaceful

When wind blows across a pond, it drags the surface of the water into waves. The wind disturbs the water and makes it turbulent. When the wind goes away, the water relaxes back to a state of tranquil equilibrium. So it is with ourselves: the wind of our thoughts, feelings, senses, and experiences can churn us up, but we can always relax back into a state of peace.

Imagine you are sitting at the edge of a pond in the fall. The air is still; the maples, ablaze, are still; and the pond is still, glassily reflecting the pastoral landscape. Imagine the stillness of the water absorbing into your mind, and your mind becoming like the mirror surface of the water. When a thought comes up, it may stir up some ripples on the surface, but then the water relaxes back to stillness.

Now imagine your body is still like the pond. Any fidgeting just ripples away and relaxes back to equilibrium. Feel your body being as tranquil as the pond: calm, easy, quiet. Sit with this peacefulness for a few effortless breaths.

Imagine your emotions being still like the pond. Any agitation settles down and dissipates out. Your emotions slow down and come to rest like the glassy surface.

Now imagine your spirit is still like the pond. Any restlessness in your spirit loosens and relaxes. See your spirit calm, cool, quiet, tranquil—like still water.

Mind, body, emotions, and spirit can all be stilled with this exercise. The calmer your pond, the clearer will be the water. The clearer the water, the more accurately you can see through it.

{ 4 } Camp David—Be Peaceful and Loving

Imagine you're having a perfectly good conversation with your coworker, and then politics comes up. You assume that he has the same political opinions as you, but within a sentence, you've realized you have one of your feet in a bees' nest.

Of course, you know for certain that your opinion on the matter is the correct one. He is clearly uninformed. There's no way any rational person could believe what he just stated, so he must not know the facts. It's time to dig into your position and educate him, regardless of the ruckus it will cause, right?

What's on Your To Be List? Even though you have a strong desire to make yourself right and your coworker wrong, you don't have "Be Right" on your list.

When you're faced with a small skirmish, the tendency is to think that because it's small, it doesn't matter so much. We believe we can create a small ruckus, have a small fight, and it's no big deal. But it's just the opposite. Allowing a small fight is plowing the ground and planting the seeds of a large fight.

Don't downplay a skirmish, escalate it. Bring it to Camp David. Imagine that you are responsible for averting nuclear war. The very fate of the planet depends on your ability to make peace in this moment, with this adversary. You are clear on your mission: not to be right, but to create peace.

Imagine yourself face to face with someone who's spouting political opinions completely opposed to yours. You can feel the anger and righteousness rising, but instead of moving into combat mode, you decide to take this one to Camp David. See yourself negotiating skillfully, with vast wisdom and understanding, with deep compassion and generosity, with stalwart conviction and firmness. See yourself coming to a peaceful settlement where you both feel heard, understood, and respected.

When you practice being loving over and over, even to your seeming adversaries, a slow and potent peace descends into your everyday life.

{ 5 } Color Concentration—Be Peaceful and Strong

To be fully relaxed, the mind must be quiet. Quieting the mind takes concentration, which is mental strength. You can build your concentration by practicing peacefully focusing on one thing. This exercise uses the colors of the rainbow as a focal point. If you find your mind wandering as you do the exercise, just smile kindly at your thoughts and gently return to the color.

Imagine the color red as vividly as you can, as if you were looking at it with your eyes open. See it all around you, quiet, serene. If anything other than red comes to mind, gently return to focusing on the color red.

After a few breaths, see the color orange, and concentrate on making it as vivid as possible. Descend through the colors of the rainbow: Red, Orange, Yellow, Green, Blue, Violet. Stay with each color for several breaths. Feel your concentration and your peace grow stronger with each breath, and with each new color. By the time you reach purple, your feelings of peace will be a strong and still as a mountain.

You may find this exercise very relaxing. Enjoy the relaxation—just remember to stay awake!

{ 6 } Flower Power—Be Peaceful and Balanced

Where there is peace, there is balance. If you don't feel balanced, if you feel like the different parts of your life are fighting one another for your attention, there is no peace. How can you restore a sense of peaceful balance in the midst of a chaotic day? Flower power.

Imagine how it feels to be a flower. How does it breathe? Easily, effortlessly. How does it greet the morning? With calm, cheerful presence. How does it weather a rainstorm? Without fear or judging, with perfect acceptance.

Imagine how it feels to be a flower, and feel the peaceful ease with which it lives. See your eyes as flowers, your hands as flowers, your heart as a flower. Enjoy the freshness.

This feeling is always available to you. With practice, you can return to it quickly when you feel tired or stressed. Then you can be refreshed by the flower that is always within you.

{ 7 } The Troll in the Closet—Be Peaceful and Courageous

Oftentimes what churns us up the most is trying to avoid confronting our fears. When fear rears its ugly head, like a troll peeking out of the bedroom closet, we frantically try shoving him back in there where we can't see him. But even if we're successful at locking him up, we still know there's a troll lurking just behind the closet door.

The path to peace is to be courageous and look at the troll. Imagine you're in your bedroom, and you see one of your fears, in the form of a troll, peeking out at you from the closet. Though you'd really like to rush over and slam the door and pretend he's not there, this time you try something different. You say, "Oh, hi there. I recognize you, you're..." then name the fear, and be sure to use heavily ironic air quotes. "You're 'My-Fear-Of-Getting-Sick.' You look kinda tired, old friend. Can I get you some milk and cookies?" You watch him sullenly shake his troll head and stomp out of the room, defeated in his mission to scare you.

Fear happens, and it's impossible to be peaceful when you're in its grip. But every time you courageously confront and care for a fear, it loses some of its hold on you. The troll gets smaller and wimpier each time you name it and offer it milk and cookies.

{ 8 } Peaceful Receiving—Be Peaceful and Grateful

You are in a constant state of peaceful receiving. Your body gratefully accepts nourishment from your food, from the air, from the sunshine. Your mind and heart receive compassion and understanding from the people who love you. Your spirit receives sustenance from your spiritual beliefs and practices.

But sometimes we aren't so skilled at receiving gratefully, and this disrupts our peace. For example, sometimes a loved one tries to help pull you out of a bad mood by offering you advice. For whatever reason, you hear the advice as criticism, and defensively reject it. All of us get defensive and resistant. But when Be Peaceful and Grateful is on Your To Be List, you can use this situation as an opportunity to practice being the way you truly want to be.

Imagine it's your birthday, and you are out to dinner celebrating with friends and family. Your best friend clinks a glass, tells the guests it's time for presents, and hands you a beautifully wrapped gift. You smile and say, from the bottom of your heart, "Thank you. I'm so grateful for all you give me, and I'm so grateful for this gift." One by one your friends and family offer you presents, and you give each one your deepest gratitude in return. Feel the peace in your heart from receiving so graciously.

Now imagine that one of your family members gives you some well-meaning but annoying advice. Instead of reacting defensively and creating more discord, you say, from the bottom of your heart, "Thank you. I'm so grateful for all you offer me, and for that piece of advice. I'll consider it." You see the situation defused, as your choice to be grateful creates a peace that settles over the both of you.

{ 9 } Peace and Quiet Practice—Be Peaceful and Bountiful

Almost every adult craves peace and quiet. We tell ourselves, "What I wouldn't give to get away from it all on some tropical island somewhere!" But peace and quiet are not so scarce that they can only be found in the Caribbean or by shutting off our entire life. Peace is infinitely abundant, present everywhere, and ready for us to enjoy at any moment.

Instead of chasing after the ideal of absolute tranquility with a fruity drink on the beach, why not get in touch with the peace and quiet that already exist within you right now? Here's a way to practice:

When you breathe in, think,
"I feel peaceful."
When you breathe out, think,
"I feel quiet."

With each in-breath, imagine the peace flowing into your mind, body and heart from the most abundant sources of peace. Imagine mountains of peace, skies of peace, oceans of peace, flowing into you and making you feel so peaceful. Because you can imagine these peaceful scenes, and recall their peace at will, they're always with you, always available to you, always just one inhalation away.

With each out-breath, imagine quiet settling more deeply into your mind, body and heart from your abundant inner sources of quiet. Quiet forests, quiet meadows, quiet lakes, all within you and available to provide you as much delicious quiet as you want with each exhalation.

You can practice being peaceful and quiet while waiting in carpool, or in the doctor's office, or between meetings. When you can connect with the limitless sources of peace and quiet that are already within you, you'll find yourself craving the beach less. You'll also find that when you do get to the beach, it will so much more peaceful and quiet than you could ever have imagined.

{ 10 } The Body Scan—Be Peaceful and Healing

Our bodies constantly communicate with us about their state: "I'm hot, cold, tense, relaxed, hungry, full..." Just as you want to be heard when you have something to say, your body also wants to be heard. If your body is trying to tell you something, and you're not listening, it will repeat itself, and start chattering at you. The only way to quiet the chatter is to listen to the body so that it will stop trying to get your attention. Listening might not make all your aches and pains disappear, but it is not possible for a body to Be Peaceful without being heard.

Imagine a heat lamp very slowly scanning your body, starting from the top of your head, and progressing very slowly down to your toes. As the heat from the lamp touches each part of your body, tune into how that part is feeling. Listen to what each body part wants to tell you, without judging. Just listen, peacefully, compassionately. Tell each part, "I hear you. I understand."

As you listen to each part of your body, you may notice it relaxing. Your job is not to make it relax, but simply to notice it. If it's tense or painful, just notice—"feel into it." You can linger longer with the uncomfortable places, letting the light of your attention radiate inward, like a healing deep heat.

You can spend fifteen to twenty minutes on this for a powerfully heal-ing experience. But you can also take any free moment during the day and just tune into your body. Maybe right before you take your first bite of lunch, you can take a deep breath and check in with how your body is do-ing. Maybe when your shoulders get tight while you're stuck in traffic, you can just listen to them for a few moments and hear what they have to say. Even just a few moments of peaceful ease starts to dissolve disease.

This is an important exercise, and not just for your own personal heal-ing. You are part of your community, so when you bring peaceful healing to yourself, you bring peaceful healing to your community.

May you Be Peaceful and Healing.

4

Be Loving—The Power to Connect

O ur breath is very precious. Every hour of
every day, it moves in and out of our lungs,
bringing oxygen to our blood and our organs,
sustaining our lives.

But what if we decided that because our
breath is so precious, we should be careful how
we use it? We should only use it in situations
that seem worthy of our breath. Why "waste" our
breath on things that seem difficult or unpleasant? Thinking like this, we might decide to hold
on to our breath to save it only for the people and
situations that feel pleasant and warm to us.

RELATED TO BE'S

Be Giving

Be Nurturing

Be Caring

Be Devoted

Be Warm

Be Kind

Be Affectionate

Be Attentive

It's a ridiculous proposition, really, because we know for a fact that
holding on to breath is destructive to life. Breath is only life-giving if we
allow it to flow in and out of us. If we are not breathing, there is no breath.
There is no life.

But of course, we do not behave this way, because our bodies know
that air—though it is precious and key to life itself—is not in limited supply. So our bodies feel free to go on breathing and breathing.

Breathing is a kind of intimate connection between ourselves and the
world. We take air outside ourselves and transform it into the life force of
our bodies. Then we take that life force and release it back to the world as air.

Love is like the breath of the soul. It is precious. It is life giving. But at the same time, it is only vital if it moves in and out of us. And love is an energy, which like air, is in unlimited supply. It is not rare. We do not need to hide it away or save it for special people or situations. We can share the energy of love freely by choosing To Be Loving.

Choosing To Be Loving is our way of connecting infinitely and intimately to the world. It is a way of taking the life-giving energy of love that sustains our hearts and turning it outward for the benefit of others, then taking the benefit of others and drawing it back in to sustain ourselves.

Loving is like breathing; we can only draw it in by giving it away.

When we first informed our friends of our decision to adopt, some people expressed concern as to whether we could love our adopted sons as much as we loved our biological daughters. The assumption they made is that love is tied to biology; that love is limited to those who share our DNA.

But love is not a substance that is transmitted through genes. Love cannot be held or contained by biology. We cannot hold love. We can be loving. We can take loving action. And loving action can carry us across oceans, both real and imagined. Loving actions can reach out and take the hands of orphans and make them into loving sons and beloved siblings, grandchildren, nephews and friends.

When you choose To Be Loving, you can connect beyond the reaches of your physical limitations. You can touch and transform the world in ways that reach beyond the places you can see with your eyes or touch with your hands.

By choosing To Be Loving, you become like breath, that becomes the air, that becomes the wind, that moves the ocean, that reaches out to touch the sands of distant shores.

The 10 How's

{ 1 } Love Yourself First—Be Loving and Free

Learn the art of loving by practicing on yourself. In order to give, you must also receive. You always can receive loving compassion by giving it to yourself. With this exercise, you can practice both being loved and being loving. The more you practice with yourself, the easier it will be to be loving and loved by other people.

Imagine yourself as a small child of four or five years old. You are tender and fragile, innocent and pure. You deserve only support, encouragement, and unconditional love. Regardless of what your actual childhood was like, regardless of what you actually received back then, you can now give yourself exactly what you want and need.

Imagine holding the four-year-old you on your lap, embracing yourself warmly, giving yourself safety and stability, surrounding yourself with acceptance and love. Stroke the child's head and say, "All is well. You are loved completely now. All is well." Sing yourself a gentle, comforting lullaby.

Now switch perspectives so that you are the child being held. Take a few moments right now and feel the love and compassion enfolding you.

This simple exercise can be profoundly healing. It's okay to feel deeply. Let whatever comes up be completely okay. Whatever comes up, comfort it, cradle it gently, sing to it sweetly.

{ 2 } The Love Shack—Be Loving and Happy

You can unlock the ecstatic happiness within love with mindful dancing. Dancing to happy music creates the chemical and energetic conditions of happiness in your body and mind. When you combine the happiness chemicals with a mental image of something you love, you are mixing up a potent love cocktail.

You infuse the love you feel with the happiness you feel, and your love becomes stronger and easier.

First, choose someone toward whom you want to be more loving. Perhaps your significant other is being difficult, or a teenager is working your last nerve, or your coworker is bugging you, and you're finding it hard To Be Loving toward them. Hold a picture of them in your mind for a moment.

If you can't do this in real life, then just imagine it. Crank up your favorite happy dance music: "Love Shack" by the B-52's would be a great one. Start dancing with as much joy as you can. While you dance, keep your mind focused on the difficult person. Imagine smiling at them, dancing your love over to them. Imagine that they are so moved by your smiling, your dancing, and your love that they also start dancing and smiling.

Nobody ever needs to know you've had this little dance party in your private Love Shack, but don't be surprised if things begin shifting right away. Music and dancing have a way of transporting emotional signals, and the love that you've sent out just might have been received.

{ 3 } The Silent Room—Be Loving and Peaceful

All of the most beloved people in your life are alive within you, right now. Memories exist in the mind as physical things: patterns of chemicals and electrical charges. Your mind and body provide a home for all the memories of shared affection. The more you bring to mind peaceful and loving memories, the more those mental circuits are strengthened.

Imagine that in your mind, there's a room where you keep your most peaceful and loving memories. How have you furnished this chamber to make it an open, warm, loving place? Imagine your beloved ones sitting peacefully on comfortable sofas and chairs. Imagine them relaxing quietly, looking around at the beautiful art you've chosen, enjoying each other's company.

Feel the delightful stillness. See your loved ones smiling peacefully at you, and at each other. No words are necessary. You all are communicating perfectly with love. Enjoy the tranquility—you are all embraced by love.

{ 4 } The Open Heart—Be Loving

If you could write a To Be List for your heart, would you put, "Be Open" or "Be Closed"? Even though most of us would like to remember to open our hearts, there are times when we forget and clam up, withholding our love. But love can't flow out of, or into, a closed heart. We need to practice opening our heart and keeping it open so that we can freely and bountifully give and receive love.

Bring one of your hands in front of you, palm up. Imagine that it represents your heart. Feel how open and free it feels. Now make a tight fist, and feel the difference. How would you like your heart to be—like the fist or the open palm? Your clenched fist is your heart when you're feeling defensive, depressed, or defeated. Now gradually unclench your fist, opening your palm, and imagining letting go of that closed feeling in your heart.

Imagine that closed feeling resting in the palm of your hand, surrounded by your understanding, your compassion, your love.

Now think of a loved one. Breathe in and clench your fist. Breathe out, and as you slowly open your palm, imagine your heart opening to that person. Imagine a compassionate, understanding love flowing out from your palm and embracing them completely.

Bring to mind the image of a stranger, perhaps someone you saw on the subway or in traffic. Breathe in and clench your fist. Breathe out and release it, offering the stranger your love and compassion. See your compassion as a ray, permeating every cell of their body, penetrating their every thought and feeling, healing what needs to be healed.

Finally, hold in your mind someone who you need to forgive, someone who you find difficult. Breathe in and clench your fist. Hold your breath for just a moment, feeling the tight, restricted, closed feeling. Breathe out, relax, and open up. Imagine understanding the root of their problems, the reason you find them so hard to be with. Let that compassionate understanding penetrate into the root cause, like the warmth of the sun penetrates a hard seed, inviting a tiny crack. Allow the crack to spread as you continue radiating your compassion.

{ 5 } An Ideal Friend—Be Loving and Strong

Strength is the container for love. If love is water, strength is the pipe through which it flows. The stronger the pipe, the more water can flow through it. When we strengthen ourselves, our capacity to mindfully abide with whatever comes—our pipeline—can handle more love flowing through it.

The strength within love is the ability to look honestly and openly at the difficult parts of life. All love will pass, as everything is impermanent, and this can be painful. The more you love, the more pain there can be when the love passes. Being mindful and aware of that pain takes strength. The more mindful you can be, the stronger you are, and the more love you can allow to flow through you. The following exercise helps you build your inner strength.

Imagine sitting down for coffee or tea with an ideal friend. This is a dear, close friend who knows you perfectly and intimately. He or she always supports you unconditionally, and wants the best for you; a wise, understanding, solid friend who's always there for you.

You start telling your friend about your life right now. Your dreams, your fears, your projects, your emotional and mental state. Imagine your friend listening with his or her whole being.

Your friend laughs at the funny parts, and gets excited with you about your hopes and dreams. When you talk about your fears, your friend is calm and knowing, and tells you it will all be okay. When you get to the sad parts, your friend reaches across the table and takes your hand, and with moist eyes just says, "I know." Your friend is strong for you, both for the easy parts and the more difficult parts.

You already are your ideal friend. You've just done this exercise all by yourself. There's no substitute for real friends, but you've just shown that you can create the energy of compassion for yourself. You are always there for you. You have within you the strength that allows love to flow freely and confidently.

{ 6 } The Walking, Talking Orchid—Be Loving and Balanced

You might be surprised at how balanced and beautiful you already are. Try giving away some of your balance and inner beauty, and you may find there's more of it than you thought. When you share your beauty with others, you are being loving and balanced, and it feels wonderful.

Imagine an orchid, stunning in its symmetry, expressing perfect balance, embodying beauty. It stands unafraid, the ideal of poise and equilibrium, harmony and loveliness.

Imagine taking the orchid into your heart. It fills you with beauty until you're overflowing. Now imagine meeting another person—a stranger on the street, or your most beloved—a person who needs some beauty and balance right now.

Imagine that you are shining the orchid's magnificence out through your eyes and into the other person's soul. You smile, and the fragrance of the orchid fills the room and lifts up their heart. You take their hand in yours and all the balance and beauty overflowing within you spills out and fills them up, too.

You are a walking, talking orchid! You have this balance and beauty in you right now, and you can share it with everyone you meet. You can walk down the street handing out flowers with your eyes and your smile.

{ 7 } The Love Bubble—Be Loving and Courageous

A prerequisite for feeling compassion is feeling safe. If your fight-or-flight system is doing its best to keep you safe from harm, your body and mind are chemically primed for self-preservation. Your system is looking for threats, not for opportunities to practice compassion. In order to practice compassion, you must first create a feeling of safety, and deactivate that alarm system.

Imagine a bubble of safety deep inside you. It is protected from all harm, and is filled only with pure love. Now see the bubble growing, as the limitless nature of the pure love expands it. See the bubble of light encircling you completely. You are surrounded by nothing but pure love, and you are completely safe.

Stay in your safe space for a few minutes, breathing in and breathing out, grateful for the perfect safety and love around you.

{ 8 } The Refreshing Rain Shower—Be Loving and Grateful

When you are Being Loving, love will flow back to you. Once you get the energy of love moving by giving, you will begin receiving it back, as sure as more air rushes in behind the wind as it blows. The more gratefully you receive it, the faster and more freely it will flow in and out.

Imagine you are walking in an open field. All of a sudden, you feel the unmistakable splash of a raindrop on your scalp. You look up, and sure enough, a light summer rain has begun to fall. You have nothing to do but welcome it. You're going to get wet, so you decide to gratefully receive the rain.

You notice that the soil is also thankful for the shower—its sun-dried cracks are drinking up the rain with a big grateful smile. The shower quickens to a downpour. The grasses and flowers in the field rejoice, their leaves dancing with the drops, their heads nodding in time with the rhythm of the rain. You decide to be as grateful as the parched field for the loving gift of the rain.

You open your mouth to the sky and drink in the rainwater. You feel it refreshing and cleansing you. You are filled with the energies of love and gratitude. You join your palms in front of you, standing in a warm shower, and are thankful for this moment.

{ 9 } Love, Inc.—Be Loving and Bountiful

Love is the business of your heart. A good business executive learns how to keep the machines well oiled, the processes efficient, and the production levels high. A good executive learns how to measure and manage all operations to the benefit of the customers and owners.

Who are the customers of your heart? Your family, your friends, your coworkers. These people all benefit when you produce love in the factory of your heart.

Imagine a beautiful organic factory in your heart. From the smokestacks, a warming light emerges. Shining from all the clean bright windows are rays of love. No matter what is delivered to this factory—pain, anger, hatred, loneliness—the magical manufacturing process transforms the raw materials into a pure, clean love.

There is no limit to the amount of love that can be manufactured in the factory of your heart. There is always more than enough. Prominently displayed in the entryway of Love, Inc. is a banner with the company motto, "Bountiful Love For All." The factory of your heart is always overflowing with love and can freely give it away.

Imagine all your customers—your loved ones—standing in front of you. They are bathed in the light of love, which is streaming out of your heart's factory.

As the owner of the business, you benefit when your customers benefit. When you provide your customers the value of being loving, they will pay for your product with their own love. This is a virtuous and bountiful business model that always succeeds in great measure.

{ 10 } The Column of Love—Be Loving and Healing

A young woman sits in her apartment, full of the pain of loneliness. It's Saturday night, and she has nowhere to go. She can't bear the idea of another noisy party or smoky bar. The parties and bars always break their seductive promises—they never deliver the real love she wants in her life.

Do you know someone who lives with the pain of loneliness? This exercise will help you heal yourself first, and then your lonely loved one, so that she can enjoy being loving and being loved in return.

When we help her heal, we gently but powerfully heal ourselves in the process. We connect with the universal field of Love, and bring its miraculous healing power into our lives.

Bring your attention back to yourself—feel yourself right where you are. Feel your feet on the floor and your back in your chair. Watch one complete inhalation. Watch one complete exhalation.

Now feel that there is a column of golden light shining down on you. It is infinite Love. Feel how it shines on every part of you—every cell in your body, every thought in your mind, every feeling in your heart. Feel how it shines a smile of complete knowing and acceptance on every part of you.

Every cell in your body is known, and accepted, by this infinite Love. Every thought that flits through your mind is known and accepted. Every feeling which ebbs and flows through your heart is known and accepted. You are bathed in this knowing, accepting, infinite Love.

Staying within the column of Love surrounding you, see your loved one who is lonely. See them in your mind as clearly as you can: see what they're wearing, see their hair and skin, their hands and feet. Send a stream of the infinite Love to them—from your heart to their heart. It knows and accepts all of the cells in their body, all of the thoughts in their mind, all of the feelings in their heart. See their face transform into a blissful smile. You can tell that they feel completely known, accepted, and loved.

See the column of infinite Love around you expanding until it encompasses you both. You can feel that this Love is everywhere, all the time, knowing and accepting everything that is. You are swimming in it. Your loved one is swimming in it. It is now healing you both, helping you to be ever more deeply loved and loving.

May you share the healing power of love.

5

Be Strong—The Power to Stand Firm

Anyone who has ever been to the gym to lift weights knows that it takes commitment and discipline to build strength. We begin with small weights, and gradually as we feel more confident, increase the weight. The more weight we can lift, the more our muscles grow. The bigger our muscles, the more energy is stored and at the ready when it is needed. Having a natural sense of our own power, we feel comfortable using it outside the gym. If we need to rearrange furniture in our home, we can count on our strength to aid us in the heavy lifting. If we want to go on a long hike through the woods to see a beautiful vista, we know our strength can carry us to our destination. If we need to bend over and pick up a hurt child, we know that we can rely on our strength to aid us in our compassion.

RELATED TO BE'S
Be Energetic
Be Solid
Be Responsible
Be Discerning
Be Decisive
Be Prudent
Be Honorable
Be Ethical
Be Trustworthy
Be Committed
Be Organized
Be Motivated

In the same way, our inner strength is what gives our hearts the energy and the power to perform the kind of emotional heavy lifting that life often requires of us. If we need to rearrange our priorities, we know that our hearts can endure the transitional process. If we seek the broad vistas of a new life goal, we know that our hearts can carry us through the long haul to our destination. If we want to be there for a friend or a colleague or a family member who is hurt and in need of our help, we know that our hearts can reach out and offer the kind of compassionate support that will bring hope and healing.

By choosing To Be Strong, we take on a kind of discipline for the heart and soul so that when our lives call upon us to lend our energy to bring about change, we know that we have deep stores of energy to draw from. We can stand firm within ourselves and know that we will not buckle under the weight of our responsibilities. We can persevere through difficulty and know that a moment will come when we will look at the remarkable vistas of our lives and smile, knowing that all the effort was worth it. We can reach out to take the hand of another who is suffering, knowing that we have the heart to soothe their pain and the wisdom to uplift their spirits.

Choosing strength enables us to bring wisdom, happiness, and love to our lives and to the lives of others through the power of our own hearts to stand firm, to move with purpose, and to uplift.

When furniture in a room needs to be moved and rearranged, we will sometimes stand at the threshold of the room and wonder how it will ever get done. There is so much shifting and changing that needs to take place. Just standing there, looking at the massive amount of work to do, we might get discouraged and never even start.

But if we know that in the end, space will be liberated and greater beauty will be revealed in that room, we gather our strength and we begin to lift and move. First we pick up the small items and then we move to the large pieces—until the room begins to take shape—sometimes in ways that we envisioned, sometimes in ways that we never could have imagined. But without faith in our strength, the change could never happen.

When we decided to adopt our older son, we did not know how we would manage this enormous transition in our family physically, financially, emotionally, or spiritually. Bringing a fourth child into our family, a child who had lived for over three years in an orphanage, was never part of our family plan. We stood at the threshold of possibility and wondered how we could possibly find the strength to begin. But all the same, we knew that we had within us the reserves of emotional and spiritual strength to overcome any challenges we might face while bringing him home and making him part of our family.

We had to choose To Be Strong for ourselves, but even more importantly, we had to choose To Be Strong for him. He did not have the reserves of strength that we had. He did not have the ability to transform his life. We did. And so we reached deep within ourselves and found that strength, not really knowing how much strength it would require, or how much effort it would take, or how long we would have to persevere.

We began by picking up the phone and saying, "yes." Yes, we would adopt this little boy and make him our son.

Our choice to be strong changed his life. It changed ours.

When you choose strength you are choosing to be a force for change.

The 10 How's

{ 1 } The Guardians of the Gates—Be Strong and Free

"Freedom is not free," intones the wise and popular bumper sticker. Sometimes we do have to stand firm to protect our freedom. Sometimes we have to stand up to those who seek to limit us. It takes strength to guard our freedom. It takes strength to envision a new future.

Imagine that you have a sacred space within you. This space is your refuge, your sanctuary. It is a space of limitless freedom: the space where you are free to choose what To Be.

Post your most watchful guards at the gates to this sanctuary. Imagine there are strong castle walls around your sacred space, and a drawbridge with a moat.

Imagine that a person from your life shows up at the gates and requests entrance. Your guards know that letting them in right now will compromise your freedom to choose what you want To Be. The guards stand firm, and calmly say, "No visitors now. Come back later." Your sentinels are strong, and the visitor is turned away.

Imagine that a troublesome thought approaches the gates of your free-dom sanctuary, perhaps a thought like, "I'm going to fail—I just know it." Your guards see the thought coming and pull up the drawbridge. They shout across the moat, "We have no need for you here—please return from whence you came!" The thought, seeing the futility of trying to breach your fortifications, slinks back into the forest.

People, thoughts, feelings, and events show up daily at freedom's gates. They may request entrance to your sanctuary, with the intent to con-trol you, manipulate you, and infringe upon your basic rights. But your guards and your castle are strong, and you will protect your freedom to choose who you want To Be, by standing firm.

{ 2 } The Gene Kelly Float—Be Strong and Happy

If you've never seen the movie *Singin' In The Rain*, treat yourself to a rental. The classic musical is sure to stimulate your sense of both strength and happiness.

Gene Kelly was one of the greatest dancers of the twentieth centu-ry and created a uniquely American style: at once graceful and athletic, grounded and weightless. He seemed to float through the most physical-ly strenuous routines, radiating aliveness and presence. When he's in a scene, it's impossible to take your eyes off him, and there's no sense trying to repress the impulse to mimic his puckish grin.

When you watch Kelly dance, you can sense the sheer muscular power it takes to make the demanding tap numbers seem so effortless. Without the tremendous physical strength, there's no way he could radiate such joy. If he was huffing and puffing, straining and draining, it wouldn't be de-lightful to watch. Strength is required for the happiness to shine through.

Imagine yourself on the set of *Singin' in the Rain*, in a starring role alongside Gene Kelly. The music swells, and the dialogue gives way to song. You crouch into the stylized choreography, beaming as you flawlessly execute the complex tap routine. You can feel the strength in your muscles supporting you. You smile at the camera with everything you've got—from soles of your tap shoes to the fedora on your perfectly coiffed head.

You can take that sense of strength and happiness and dance through the rest of your day. Maybe your puckish grin will rub off on someone else!

{ 3 } Do Less Stronger—Be Strong and Peaceful

Sometimes we find ourselves racing around our lives: We have so many demands on our time, so many good things we want to do, that we sprint from one activity to another without pausing to enjoy any of them. The frenetic pace scatters our concentration and weakens our efforts.

Instead, practice being strong and peaceful by doing less, but doing it all stronger. But what to do less of? It all seems so pressing, so urgent. Perhaps you've tried prioritizing, and found even that to be draining: how do you know if number eight or number nine on your priority list is more important?

The trick is to only do number one on your list, and don't worry about anything lower down on the list. If you're always giving your all to the most important thing on your list, practicing being strong and peaceful, the quality of everything you do will soar. Number nine on your list no longer matters, because you know that if and when number nine becomes number one, you'll do it with impeccable integrity and focus.

Imagine that you're at work and you see an opportunity that you know is truly important. You know that if you accomplished this one goal superbly well, it would yield great results. Imagine committing to do your best at this task. Feel the feeling of knowing in your heart that this is going to go exceptionally well, because you're going to put everything you've got into it.

You're going to do it with strength and with peace.

Now see another task trying to enter your to-do list. Perhaps someone sent you an E-mail with some request for your time. Visualize yourself as a boulder, and this E-mail as a ping-pong ball bouncing off the boulder. See yourself standing strong, and gently, peacefully, saying, "No. My priorities are clear right now."

You can do the same with the kids' extracurricular activities or to balance the competing demands of work and home. Commit with the strength of a mountain to what you know is important, and stand firmly and peacefully as all the rest just comes and goes.

{ 4 } Inner Compassion—Be Strong and Loving

When you practice being loving, you are allying yourself with one of the strongest forces in the universe: Love. The very act of offering unconditional love strengthens and fortifies you. When you choose To Be Loving, you are unquestionably choosing to be a force for channeling goodness into the world.

It doesn't matter if you're offering love to yourself, another person, or even an inanimate object—it's all good—but the highest leverage you have is with yourself. Being compassionate and understanding toward yourself will always strengthen you in the most profound and healing ways.

Imagine sitting in a rocking chair as your wisest, most loving self. Now imagine holding in your hands your favorite part of yourself, like it was a little marble. Maybe it's your nurturing spirit, or your organized mind, or your creativity. Send your little marble unconditional love. See where it came from. Smile at it kindly and knowingly.

Now imagine holding in your hands something you don't like so much about yourself. Maybe it's one of your fears, doubts, worries or character weaknesses. It's also a little marble. Offer it your understanding: "Little marble of [fear, doubt, worry...], it's okay. I see that you're there, and I understand you. We've lived together for some time now, and I know you very well." Send it unconditional compassion. Look deeply into it, and without trying to fix it or deny it, see where it came from. Smile at it with a kind and knowing smile. Nothing has to happen or change. Let whatever happens happen, and you will emerge with a new bit of inner strength.

You may want to move back and forth between feeling compassion for your favorite parts of your self and your least favorite parts, to strengthen your unconditional love.

{ 5 } Pick up the Dumbbell—Be Strong

If it was easy to stay on Your To Be List, everyone would do it. It takes strength to choose to do your daily tasks with meaning. It takes strength to stay mindfully engaged with what you find most meaningful in your life. It takes strength to resist getting distracted by all your noisy, urgent to-do's and forgetting your silent, but vitally important To Be's.

Thankfully, you only need enough strength to re-engage in this very moment. You have all the strength you need to mindfully bring one To Be to whatever you're doing. Don't worry about making your whole day meaningful, just the one to-do that's in front of you right now.

Imagine you have a set of dumbbells collecting dust in the corner of your room. (Maybe you don't have to imagine?) They're there in plain sight, yet you walk by them dozens of times a day, barely noticing them except for an occasional twinge of guilt.

Imagine that this time when you walk by, you decide, "I'm just going to pick up this one dumbbell and lift it once. That's better than nothing." You take hold of it and hoist it above your head, with strength, with power, with victorious determination.

Now envision engaging with Your To Be List in the same way. Instead of just walking by "Be Grateful" and letting it collect dust in the corner, you decide to pick it up like it was a dumbbell and lift it over your head. Every time you do any task on your to-do list, from taking out the garbage to returning a phone call, it's like walking past your To Be. Will you pick it up, lift it once, and get stronger?

{ 6 } The Subway Handrail—Be Strong and Balanced

Dynamic balance is tenuous. You're always shifting and moving to stay in balance, intuitively adapting to changing conditions. Being Balanced is a wobbly endeavor.

To stay steady, you need to focus on something unmoving. You need the strength of focus.

Imagine you're riding a subway, and it's standing room only, so you're standing. As the car pulls out of the station and bounces up to full speed, it begins to lurch and sway like a rowboat on the open ocean. No matter how much you adjust your footing or your center of gravity, you know that you've just got to hold onto something or you're going to topple over.

You find a few spare inches on the handrail overhead, and suddenly your balance picture is transformed. With two feet on the ground and a steady anchor point over your head, you are remarkably stable. You know that no matter which direction the subway car lurches, you'll be able to adjust, stand firm, and avoid crashing over onto your neighbor.

What's the focal point in your life that would help you balance right now? What's the unmovable principle that can help steady you through the bumps you may experience today? Perhaps it's your faith. Or perhaps it's making time for proper exercise, or staying connected to a loved one, or taking time out for relaxation. Maybe you have a sense of mission, or a big exciting life goal, or a set of values that's your unmoving focal point.

Whatever it is, reach out and take hold of it firmly, keep your eye on it, and draw strength and balance from your unwavering focus.

{ 7 } The Wildflower on the Rock—Be Strong and Courageous

On life's journey, sometimes the going gets tough. We all have times when we're afraid, overwhelmed, exhausted, resistant, or just defeated. That's where strength and courage come in to pick you up and get you moving again. Strength is the power to take the next step, and courage is the willingness to take it, even though you really don't feel like it.

Imagine that you're hiking up a mountain. The path winds through dense growth, so you can only see a few paces in front of you. It's been uphill for what seems like years, and you're exhausted from the exertion. You know there's a breathtaking vista up ahead, but right now, you just feel out of breath. You pause for a moment to find the strength and courage to take the next step.

In that pause, a scraggly little wildflower growing out of the rock face catches your eye. It is so fresh, jaunty, and cheeky, that you burst into a smile.

You take a deep breath and feel the solidity and strength of the mountain below you, supporting you in your journey. You look over at the wildflower and breath in its freshness, its naïve audacity. You decide that if this fragile seedling can bloom on a rock face, you can take one more step. You come back to the present moment, and with strength and courage, put one foot in front of the other. Then, staying in the present moment, you do it again.

When we reach a steep and uncertain uphill on our life's path, sometimes the only way to go is to take it one step at a time. If you take each step, in its own perfect timing, with freshness, solidity and mindful courage, not only will you will get to the breathtaking vista, but you will have enjoyed the journey.

{ 8 } The Gratty Awards—Be Strong and Grateful

What you focus on grows, so why not choose to focus on your strengths? The more you can be grateful for all the strengths you have right now, the stronger you'll become.

Imagine that you're an accepting an award for Lifetime Achievement in Strength and Gratitude (maybe the show is called the "Gratty Awards"). Give an acceptance speech, and thank all of your strengths, as if each strength was a person who contributed to your success, like your agent, your publicist, etc. Imagine a short blurb about why you're grateful for that strength, and how it contributed to you winning the award. What has each strength done for you?

For example, "There are so many strengths I'd like to thank—I can't possibly remember them all, so I prepared some notes... I'd like to thank my Excellent Communication Skills for helping me relate to so many different kinds of people. I want to thank my Intuitive Sense for always steering me in the right direction. And, of course, I'd be nowhere without my Caring Nature, which has been with me through thick and thin all these years, helping me care for all the other people around me... I couldn't have done it without all of you. I love you all—thank you and good night!"

Unlike the real awards shows, there is no time limit. Thank as many of your strengths as you can. They'll appreciate it, and you'll grow stronger and more grateful.

{ 9 } Moving Day—Be Strong and Bountiful

Strength runs throughout your body, your mind, your heart, and your spirit. It has to be there—life takes strength. Just by virtue of the fact that you are alive right now, you have more strength than you need.

Even though you have as much strength as you need, you may still want more to support you in your life. How do you build bountiful strength? The first step is to imagine it. With crystal clarity, imagine being exactly the way you wish to be. Once you are clear on the goal—bountiful strength—your thoughts, words, and actions will lead you to build the strength you desire.

Imagine that you are helping a friend move. You are loading their furniture and their boxes into a truck. Imagine you have all the strength you need to lift and carry the heavy loads. Feel the strength in your back, your legs, and your arms as you easily hoist the book boxes and ferry them to the truck.

On your way back into the house, you see your friend struggling with a particularly heavy and awkward table, and you rush over and help them out. You easily get the table into the truck, as you have strength to spare.

Now imagine that "strength to spare" feeling in your emotional life. Imagine that you're able to hold heavy emotions like they were book boxes. When fear or sadness materializes in your life, you have all the strength you need to carry them to where they need to go, and gently unload them.

Because you have more than enough emotional strength, you can help out a friend who is struggling with a heavy burden. Who would that be? Imagine that you take one corner of their fear or sadness and just help them hold it until they're ready to gently put it down.

You can also visualize yourself having more than enough mental strength, or spiritual strength. Once you've seen it clearly, you'll know the perfect next step to build it.

{ 10 } Ocean Cleansing—Be Strong and Healing

We all have little hurts and big hurts—everything from a tightness in the shoulders to a bitterness in the soul. The more we heal the big and little hurts in our lives, the stronger we can be. When part of us is not at ease, it talks to us, sometimes quite insistently, and tries to capture our attention. If we don't help it heal by giving it our full awareness, it just gets louder and more demanding. The more we can quiet these cries for our attention, the more strength of concentration we will have available.

Imagine you're standing on the beach, preparing to wade into the ocean. You traveled many miles to get here, and you're road weary: cramped, sticky, fuzzy. As you wade into the ocean, you feel the waves beginning to wash away all your tension. They crash over your feet and ankles, relaxing them, healing them. Then they wash around your calves, knees, and thighs, taking all your cares out to sea. The waves massage your belly and torso, loosening any chronic tightness you're holding there. You dive in and feel the salty water gently buffeting you, cleansing you, healing you.

Now you're comfortably immersed in the rolling waves. You hold your breath and bob on the surface, letting the ocean swish you back and forth, like you were in a giant washing machine. Imagine your skin letting in all the healthy, revitalizing nutrients from the ocean and letting out any impurities. All the tensions in your body, mind, and spirit all are swept up into the waves and washed away. You feel yourself at one with the vast healing power of the ocean.

May you heal your big and little hurts with strength and power.

6

Be Balanced—The Power to Adjust

Most of the time, when we say we want balance in our lives, we're looking for a magic formula to follow. We want to balance our work and our personal lives. We want to balance the time we spend caring for others with the time we spend taking care of ourselves. We think that once we evenly distribute our time to the people that need it, and our energy to the tasks that require it, balance will be achieved

RELATED TO BE'S

Be Adaptable

Be Stable

Be Poised

Be Even-tempered

Be Intuitive

Be Beautiful

once and for all. We will not have to think about it or worry about it any more. It's just a matter of sound scheduling: doling out the right amount of time and energy to the right people in the right proportions.

But a balance that relies on scheduling out solid blocks of time is very fragile. It is like a child's block structure: because it is built from solid, inflexible components, it is always teetering on the edge of collapse. The rigid inflexibility of the blocks is the very cause of its undoing. A block structure, no matter how finely balanced, is always just one block away from being a pile of rubble on the floor.

We have all had times when our day seemed balanced just as we had planned. Just the right amount of work. Just the right amount of play. Just enough time for others. Just enough time for ourselves. And then that one misplaced block gets piled on top and the whole structure we created begins to teeter: our car breaks down, or our child gets sick, or a coworker needs us to fill in for them at the last minute. Suddenly the balanced day we worked so hard to perfect feels like the block structure that came tumbling down. We find ourselves on the floor, picking through the rubble, trying to find our enjoyment of life.

Real balance is not rigidly constructed. Real balance requires us to be open and flexible.

If you've ever tried balancing on one foot, you know that in order to stay upright you need to constantly adjust your position. If you begin falling to your right, you might need to shift your weight to your left hip. You may need to turn your knee this way or your foot that way. You may need to recruit your arms into service. Once you have regained your balance and have a good sense of where your weight and your limbs should be, you might find that you can stand on one foot making only micro-adjustments. The more you practice balancing, the less you will wobble.

Balancing on one leg is an intuitive process. When you balance, you don't think, "Oh, I am falling forward, to my right, I had better shift more weight to my left heel and hip and put my arms out." Your body knows intuitively how to keep itself upright.

If adapting intuitively is the first key to balance, the other key is choosing a point of focus and keeping your eyes trained on that spot. It gives you an unmoving point of reference. Even while your body is teetering and adjusting, your focal point remains constant and stable.

Choosing To Be Balanced in life requires that we stay focused on the things we value most, while at the same time being open to shifting our thoughts or adjusting our course of action.

As the two of us were preparing to travel to Kazakhstan to adopt our two boys, the tragedy of September 11 was like a hurricane-force gale that blew into our well-assembled, well-balanced lives, threatening to topple everything we had planned and hoped for. By keeping our hearts and minds focused on what we valued most—being good parents and caring for the well-being of all four of our children—we were able to find a measure of balance in a turbulent time.

Balance—the power to adjust—let us intuitively shift our thoughts and adjust our course of action so that we could keep moving forward.

Life is unpredictable, to say the least. And there are times when you may feel you are about to tumble and fall to the ground. But by choosing To Be Balanced, you will be able to maintain your focus on what matters most, and intuitively shift and change to meet the needs of the moment.

With balance, you not only stay upright and poised, you can move through the world with grace and certainty, knowing that you can meet whatever challenges life brings.

The 10 How's

{ I } The Bucking Bronco—Be Balanced and Free

Some days, life feels like you're trying to ride a bucking bronco. You're tossed from crisis to crisis. You're jerked back and forth by competing priorities at work, at home, and in your personal life. You're hanging on for dear life, just trying to make it to the end of the day in one piece.

What does it take to regain balance and freedom on your bucking bronco days? Let go, shake it off, and breathe. This exercise helps you rehearse all three steps, so it's easier in real life.

Imagine you're on the back of a wildly bucking horse. It's doing everything in its power to throw you off, and you, in turn, are hanging on with all your might. Just as you're beginning to think you've been beaten, you realize that you're the one who is holding on, not the horse. The horse is just bucking—you're the one who is trying to stay on his back.

So you let go. You slide off, landing on two feet on the ground. Visualize the horse shaking it off, then calming down and walking into its stable. Feel your legs planted firmly into the ground. You, too, shake it off, like a dog after a bath. A shake is a natural "reboot" for your nervous system, getting rid of the stress of holding on for dear life. Then take a deep breath, place your hands over your lower abdomen, and let out a sigh. Stay centered for a few moments, watching the rise and fall of your lower abdomen.

Remember this exercise when you have one of those bucking bronco days. Remember to release your grip on the upsetting thoughts and feelings you're having—they are not you, they're just a horse you're trying to ride. Remember to let go, shake it off, and breathe.

{ 2 } The No-Cigarette Break—Be Balanced and Happy

Cigarette breaks would be so healthy if it weren't for the cigarettes. Every couple of hours or so, you get outside into the fresh air, maybe with a friend, and take some deep breaths for ten minutes. Nothing else. Smokers come back from their breaks refreshed and ready for business, and it's not entirely due to the nicotine.

So, take a no-cigarette break.

Imagine you're at work, and you're overloaded to the point of diminishing returns; you're neither balanced nor happy. Imagine saying to your coworkers, "Alright, I'm going for a no-cigarette break—anyone want to join me?" You and a friend make your way outside, and even though it's raining, you stand under an awning. You and your friend start by taking about a dozen deep breaths. You breathe in the moist fragrant air, and you breathe out a smile, with great enjoyment. Nothing else—no E-mails on your Blackberry, no planning or scheming, no cell phones. You just enjoy whatever sensations come your way.

After your breathing, you chat with your friend about their family for a few minutes, then head back in, feeling refreshed, connected, balanced and happy. You're so relaxed and happy that your other coworkers wonder what exactly you've been smoking out there, and secretly vow to join you next time.

{ 3 } The Intuition Tube—Be Balanced and Peaceful

The mantra of being balanced and peaceful is, "Go with the flow." Your intuition will tell you where the flow is, and how to go with it. Biologically speaking, your intuition exists to process vast amounts of (mostly subconscious) information and to give you good advice. Your intuition has no biological incentive to unbalance or upset you by giving you bad advice. If you follow the flow of your intuition, life suddenly becomes easy, as if you had stopped trying to swim upstream.

Imagine you're floating in an inner tube on a river. As long as you are sitting in it and relaxing, you naturally and effortlessly go with the flow. If you were to try to stand up, you would find yourself fighting for balance, not at all aware of the natural flow of the river or the beauty all around you. If you were to try to make your inner tube go upstream, you would be paddling frantically, not at all peaceful. It's much harder to achieve a goal that is not in harmony with the direction your environment is powerfully moving in.

Instead of standing up and getting unbalanced, or thrashing your way upstream, you decide to just relax into the inner tube. Your mind settles, and you begin to really enjoy the peaceful flow of the river. Dangling your hands and feet into the water, you notice how the river seems still around you, even though you're moving at a fair clip. You take a deep breath and sigh, "Ahh—this is the life!"

The next time you face a choice in your daily routine, you can consult this still, peaceful, balanced, flowing place in you. Relax into the inner tube of intuition and see what happens!

{ 4 } The Warm Blanket—Be Balanced and Loving

Being loving, understanding and compassionate opens the channel between you and your intuition, so that you can hear more clearly what you need to do to stay balanced in the moment. Being loving creates a safe and still space where your intuition can speak freely.

Imagine yourself sitting in a cozy chair in front of a window. Though there's a chilly rain outside, you feel completely safe, dry, and comfortable. You draw a warm blanket around you, and the heat from the blanket sinks into your body, dissolving any tension and filling you with love. It sinks into your muscles, into your bones, into your heart, and into your gut. See yourself enfolded by a blanket of warmth, compassion and understanding. Any thought or feeling that comes up—whether comfortable or not—is embraced by the loving warmth from the blanket around you.

In this accepting, loving space, you ask your intuition, "What would be balancing for me right now?" Smile at whatever comes up, and enfold it with the warmth of love.

{ 5 } Feet on the Ground—Be Balanced and Strong

When you begin a sequence of yoga or Tai Chi moves, it's common to start with a posture to help ground you. When preparing to practice poses that challenge your balance, it helps to start by getting into a very stable, solid posture and feel the balance that comes from that strength.

In yoga, for example, there is a pose called "Mountain Pose," or "*Tadasana*," in which you practice just standing on two feet, solid as a mountain. But you don't have to be in yoga class to be strong and balanced; you can do it wherever you are, as many times as you want throughout the day.

Right where you are, feel into the places where your body weight is supported. Assuming you are sitting in a chair, feel the backs of your thighs, and how they are in contact with the seat of the chair. Just pose the question: how do they feel right now? Feel your feet on the floor. Is there some grounding, some stability there? Move your attention to your back, resting against the back of the chair. Can you feel some solidity and support in your back?

Whenever you need some balance during the day, try checking in with your feet. When you place your attention on the parts of your body that are supporting your weight, your mind gets reunited with your body, and you draw strength and balance from the support.

{ 6 } The Oracle in the Forest—Be Balanced

The first key to being balanced is getting in touch with your intuitive sense of what feels right in the present moment. Sometimes that's easier said than done, especially when you're already feeling off balance. This exercise will help you get back in touch with your intuitive guidance.

Imagine that you're walking on a trail through the woods. You've come here looking for guidance and solace from the turbulence and stress in your life. With each step, you leave your troubles a little further behind. With each step, your mind calms. You find yourself walking more slowly, breathing more deeply.

Up ahead you see a clearing. As you approach the clearing, you feel a sense of peace wash over you. You know that here, all is well. In the center of the clearing, you become aware of an enlightened Being, and you sense that this Presence is a source of limitless love and wisdom.

You approach with reverence, and ask for guidance. "What's the wisest way for me to come back into balance right now?" Listen to the reply with gratitude and knowing. Bow with thanks, and gently return to your day, with certainty and faith that you have heard correctly.

{ 7 } The Beam—Be Balanced and Courageous

In the middle of a rocky day, you can use balance and courage together to make your way through it with meaning. Being courageous gives you the ability to face your troubles and keep moving anyway. Being balanced gives you the ability to tune into your intuition and use it to make small, wise corrections from moment to moment.

Imagine that you are at one end of a balance beam. Just as you step on, a question crosses your mind: "What if I fall?" See this fear in front of you, almost as if it were another person on the other end of the beam. Look it squarely in the eye and say, "If I fall, then I'll get back on." And step onto the beam.

As you're crossing, using your body's intuition to guide you, another thought appears: "I don't know what I'm doing! I've never been trained in this—I'm going to fall!" See the fear in front of you, and answer, "I'm just fine right now. Thank you for trying to protect me, but I've got it handled." Then take your next step, in perfect balance. See yourself walking the entire beam, with courage and balance.

When you get to that point in your day when you don't know how you're going to make it through, remember how courageous and balanced you felt on the beam in this exercise. Then take your next step.

{ 8 } Traffic Thanksgiving—Be Balanced and Grateful

Our days are filled with things that seem designed to knock us off balance.

A vase breaks and, mysteriously, none of your kids did it. A colleague drops the ball at work and won't own up to it. You have to miss your workout again because the boss wants you at an early meeting. Often, what knocks us off balance is a sense of entitlement. We mistakenly believe that life owes us children, colleagues and bosses who act exactly the way we want them to act. When they don't, we feel ripped off, and off balance.

You can neutralize entitlement with its opposite—gratitude. When you're in a state of gratitude, it's impossible for entitlement to rock your boat. It's hard to remember to be grateful in the moment, unless you're in practice, which is what this exercise is for.

Imagine you've been stuck in traffic for twenty minutes, and someone zips by in the breakdown lane. Not fair, right? Just as you start to formulate a lecture to them in your mind, you remember you have a choice. You're going to be in traffic for the next few minutes, and while you're sitting there, you're going to be practicing being something. What will you practice? You can practice being upset, ripped-off and self-righteous, or you can practice being grateful and balanced. You decide the latter would be more enjoyable, and start looking around for things to be grateful for. You decide to have a little Thanksgiving ceremony right there in the middle of traffic.

"I'm grateful I have a car. I'm grateful that the car is not in the shop. I'm grateful that I have gas in the car. I'm grateful that I can drive. I'm grateful that I have two hands to steer, and two eyes to see. I'm grateful that I can see the beautiful sky. I'm grateful that I can breathe freely..." Just let it flow, feeling grateful for each thought, feeling and observation.

After just a few minutes of this, you feel much more balanced. And, with one last gesture of thanks giving, you feel grateful for the balance.

{ 9 } Pumpkin Diversity—Be Balanced and Bountiful

Imagine a pumpkin, full and ripe at the end of autumn. The pumpkin is composed of many diverse pieces: the seeds, strings, skin, meat, stalk, leaves, roots, etc. Inside each one of these parts of the pumpkin, there is even more diversity; for example, the seeds have an outer shell and an inner nutritive kernel. We could keep zooming in, down to the cellular level, and even into the atomic level, and find more and more diversity, all in perfect balance.

The pumpkin is bursting with life, and with individual components all working in harmony, all making subtle adjustments to stay in balance with each other.

So are we all. Imagine all the many parts of you—your thoughts, your feelings, your history, your bones, your muscles—all working together in perfect harmony to create the superstructure called You. Feel yourself teeming with abundant life. All the 50 trillion cells in your body are individually alive, and all are making subtle adjustments to stay in balance at every moment. What a bountiful and balanced being you are!

{ 10 } The Table—Be Balanced and Healing

Visualize a table with four strong, solid legs. If any one of those legs gets weakened or damaged, the table loses its balance. To keep the table balanced, we need to tend to the health of its four legs.

So it is with ourselves. Our four "table legs" are the mind, the body, the emotions, and the spirit. The healthier and stronger those four legs, the richer, fuller and more balanced can be our response to life.

All of our supporting legs are connected to the same table, so strengthening one helps the entire table balance better. For example, proper exercise clearly strengthens the body, but it also nourishes the mind, emotions and spirit. It's the same with nutrition, time spent in Nature, meditation, rest, meaningful work, loving companionship, prayer, and relaxation. If it's good for one leg of the table, it's good for the whole table.

Imagine yourself walking around the table of your life. Take a look at each of the four legs in turn. Body, mind, emotions, spirit—which table leg needs the most attention from you right now? What is the one small change you can make to bring more health and wholeness to that supporting leg? What will be the benefits to the other legs, and to the whole table?

May you easily bring balance and healing to yourself, and to all those around you.

7

Be Courageous—The Power to Act Anyway

When we think of courage, we think of heroes. We think of the firefighters who selflessly rushed into the World Trade Center on September 11. We think of the profound faith of Martin Luther King, Jr. marching through Montgomery. We think of six-year-old Ruby Bridges walking to school in New Orleans in 1960, surrounded by U.S. Marshals as a throng of jeering protesters screamed at her, spat at her, and threatened her life.

RELATED TO BE'S

Be Patient

Be Enduring

Be Assertive

Be Confident

Be Expressive

Be Trusting

These people are cultural icons because of their willingness to serve selflessly in the face of danger, oppression, and hatred.

We think of heroes as fearless. But to think of them that way is to deny them an essential vulnerability that makes them so human and their stories so relatable and important to us. If heroes did not experience fear, then their ability to face obstacles would not seem so remarkable. Heroes are heroes, not because they are without fear, but because they move forward despite their fear. They move through their fear because they know that on the other side of fear is a worthy goal: the affirmation of the value of each and every human life.

We all have the potential to be heroes. We may live with fear, but we also have the potential to move through our fear to affirm what we know to be inherently valuable and deeply important in life. And in order to bridge the divide between fear and affirmation, we need to choose To Be Courageous.

To Be Courageous does not mean that we have to rush into a burning building or break down racial barriers. Being courageous may mean picking up the phone and apologizing to a friend. It may mean speaking up in a meeting. Being courageous may mean going back to school or starting a new career. It may mean ending a relationship or reaching out to start a new one. Perhaps we are not laying down our lives. Maybe we are laying down our pride, or our fear of rejection, or a familiar but self-destructive mindset. But we must also see that by moving forward with courage, we are affirming something much greater than that we might sacrifice.

Choosing To Be Courageous is not a choice to be foolhardy or dismissive of fear. Our fear is there for a very good reason. It tells us that something important (whether that is our sense of self, or our social standing, or our safety) is at risk. We do well to pay attention to what our fear is telling us. But at the same time, we can't let our actions be dictated by our fear. We can acknowledge our fear and understand why it is there. We can even thank our fear for trying to protect us, but in the end we must keep our eyes on the prize, knowing that though fear may tug at our coattails, something larger and grander is beckoning to us to step forward into a greater future.

Our family, our neighborhood, and our circle of close friends felt very fearful about our traveling in the wake of September 11. We were frightened as well. There was good reason to feel afraid. But all the same, there was a greater sense of meaning and purpose at stake for us: Our belief that every child deserves a family. There was a promise we made to two children who were waiting for us. And there was a belief that we were put on this earth to be something more than just safe and comfortable in our lives.

When you choose To Be Courageous, you are choosing to acknowledge the fear that seeks to protect you—and at the same time you reach out to embrace the purpose that seeks to enlarge you.

The 10 How's

{ I } The Baby Bird—Be Courageous and Free

You are free when you let go of your attachments to the things that are keeping you stuck—the doubt, the fear, the confusion, the procrastination. But there's a reason you're hanging onto those things: they're familiar and comfortable. They may be evils, but at least they're known evils, versus unknown evils! It takes courage to let go of what's familiar, even if it's keeping you stuck.

So, what is keeping you stuck? Perhaps it's an unhealthy relationship, or an eating habit, or a pattern of worst-case thinking, or a refusal to offer forgiveness. What would be most freeing for you to let go of?

Imagine you're a baby bird in a nest. Your mother has provided you with a steady nourishment of worms and grubs (yum!), and now the time has come for you to venture out on your own. You know you have wings, and you know that in theory they'll keep you up in the air, but you've never tried them out. With some nudging from Mama Bird, you teeter to the edge of the nest. Visualize the nest as the place in your life where you've been stuck. You look back over your shoulder one last time at the nest that kept you safe. Then you jump.

Feel yourself opening your wings wide and catching the air beneath them. You swoop down, gathering speed, and then soar up again, with power and ease. Exhilarated, you realize that you can do it—you really can fly! As you flap up to the treetops, you look back at the nest with a new perspective. You feel grateful for the safety it provided you for so long, and proud of yourself for being courageous enough to jump out and test your wings.

The more you rehearse letting go with courage and freedom, the easier it will become.

{ 2 } Monsters Versus Clowns—Be Courageous and Happy

Facing your fears doesn't have to be all scary and heavy. There's no International Committee on Fear that says you have to react to fear with more fear. The only laws about how you react to your thoughts and feelings are the ones you yourself have enacted.

So, what if you could choose to react to fear with...say...clowns?

Imagine one of your fears is a monster. Pick a specific fear that's bothering you lately, like running out of money, getting sick, or losing something you love. Visualize it as one of the brightly colored, fuzzy monsters from popular kids entertainment. And give it a name, like Harriet.

Harriet peeks her googly head out from around a corner and says, "Rrraaaagggghhh!" Obviously trying to scare you. Not working.

You bust out an oversized toy plastic whistle and sound the alarm. A tiny little VW Bug circles in, and out of it pops a miniature squadron of clowns. The first clown approaches Harriet and squirts her with a trick lapel flower. Harriet, clearly taken aback, wipes the water out of her eye. The second clown runs up and tweaks Harriet's nose, which makes a honking sound, like, "Ga-OO-gah!" After the third clown blows up a balloon sword and starts jabbing Harriet in the tummy, she gets disgusted and ambles off.

It is perfectly courageous to face your fear by lightening it up. There's nothing like a smile to sap the power of a scary thought.

{ 3 } Peace News Network (PNN)—Be Courageous and Peaceful

There are plenty of stories about suffering in the world. These stories are tempting to consume, worry about, and spread. For some reason, it's natural for us to want to focus on this kind of news. But we must courageously resist, if we want to be peaceful.

By choosing which stories to consume and spread, you are not ignoring or suppressing the harsh realities of life. You can be aware that the harsh realities exist without getting overwhelmed by them. You can't create peace by dwelling in distress. The best way you can care for the discord in life is to build up your reserve of peace. Surround yourself with stories of peace, and direct your mind and body toward peace.

Imagine that you are the Producer of the popular new Peace News Network (PNN). In front of you is a vast bank of television monitors with live feeds from all the breaking news stories worldwide. Your job is to sift through all the potential stories and select which ones to air on PNN.

The stories reflect the whole range of the human experience: amusing, enlightening, horrific, uplifting, depressing, touching, wondrous, painful, heroic. Imagine courageously viewing all the difficult stories, and acknowledging them, but deciding not to air them. Imagine selecting the ones you'd like to broadcast to your audience in order to inspire feelings of peace in them.

You call to the engineer, "Switch to Camera 39—the story of a man volunteering to bring meals to his elderly neighbor. Wow—that's inspiring. Now switch to Camera 2—the story of a young girl standing up to a bully for her friend. How hopeful."

This is actually what you're doing all day every day. You are your own broadcast network, and you touch many people every day with your words, your feelings, your expressions, and your actions. Which stories will you choose to air?

{ 4 } The Child on the Playground—Be Courageous and Loving

Imagine you are on an elementary school playground. Over by the swing set, a little girl is playing tag. In what seems like slow motion, she trips and skins her knee. Your heart flies out to her, and you rush over to pick her up and dust her off.

In this instant, you are her primary caregiver. She needs you to acknowledge that she is in pain, and offer her compassionate support. She needs you to tell her, "I know it hurts. You'll be okay. I'll help you. Come on—let's wash off that boo-boo and give it a Band-Aid."

When you stumble and fall in your life, you become the child on the playground. You are in pain, afraid and alone. Imagine yourself coming to the rescue, racing across the schoolyard with courage and compassion, Band-Aids in hand. You can say to yourself, "I know it hurts. You'll be okay. I'll help you. Come on—let's wash off that boo-boo and give it a Band-Aid."

What Band-Aid would make your boo-boo feel better right now?

{ 5 } The Rock in the Storm—Be Courageous and Strong

Imagine you are a boulder at the tip of a rugged peninsula jutting out into the open ocean. There's a storm brewing, and you can tell it's going to get rough. Even now, the waves are gathering strength, breaking up against you with more and more force. You begin to worry that when the full storm hits, it may be the one that finally dislodges you from your comfortable resting place and tosses you onto the rocky coast, shattering you into pieces.

Just before you start a downward spiral into worry, you catch yourself, and pull out Your To Be List. You decide to Be Strong and stand firm against the buffeting waves. You feel your stable seat, you feel how solid you are all the way through, you feel sturdy and stalwart. You resolve that no matter what happens, you will be strong. Even if the worst should come, and you are shattered into tiny rocks, you will still stay strong as you continue your journey onward toward your inevitable destination: sand. Your resolution relaxes you and helps you return to the present moment, withstanding another crash of saltwater without fear.

As you face your fear of the worst possible outcome—losing your current form entirely and splintering into pieces—you develop courage. As you stand firm against the surf, you develop strength.

Being courageous and strong together builds incredible power and integrity that you can use to create the good things you want in your life.

{ 6 } A Voice from the Future—Be Courageous and Balanced

When you trust your intuition, you'll have the courage you need at every moment. Your intuition is an immensely sophisticated information processor. It takes in millions of signals from the environment every second, and has access to untold billions of bits of data from your life experience.

Some believe it taps into the collective unconscious or even a source of divine wisdom. Your intuition collates all this information together and whispers guidance in your ear about your best next move.

If you decide, "I know that my intuition is the best tool I have to guide me, and I hereby resolve to trust my intuition," you will always be making the best decision you can right at the moment. If you always know you're making the best decision possible for you right now, you'll have all the courage you need.

Sit solidly in your chair, and let your mind quiet down for three breaths. Imagine that in a chair across from you sits... you, as an eighty-year-old woman or man. You can see that the eighty-year-old you has accumulated a deep reservoir of wisdom over the years. The senior You smiles knowingly and says, "Hello, dear—it's good to see you. What can I help you with?"

Ask your elder self, "What's the very next thing on my life's path right now? What do I need to learn, do or be?" There's no need to inquire about your grand problems, the only question is the next right action. Imagine that the wise old You grins as if fondly remembering back to the days you're in now and answers you with the perfect next thing for you to do. Express your thanks to your future self for the supportive wisdom.

{ 7 } A Helping Hand—Be Courageous

Sometimes we all just need a helping hand. When things seem overwhelming, more than we can handle, we need a way out, a way up. Despite the self-reliant mantra, "pull yourself up by your bootstraps," it's actually impossible to do in reality. Sometimes when we're in a hole, bootstraps just won't do it—we need someone at the top of the hole with a pulley and a rope.

Perhaps the most courageous thing we can do when we're in a hole is to call for help. Asking for help is looking squarely at our own limitations and deciding to take action anyway. We say, "I see the limitations, but I'm going to move forward anyway! I just need some help to do it."

Imagine that you've fallen into a hole, and the sides are too tall and steep for you to climb out. Bring to mind one of your fears or limiting beliefs to be the hole. Imagine that you've been down there a while, tugging at your own bootstraps, and have just realized that it doesn't look like you're going to get out by yourself. Instead of giving up or panicking, bring your palms to your heart in gratitude for the help you are about to receive, and then put your arms up into the air with a silent request for help.

As soon as your hands are over your head, you feel your wrists grasped gently and firmly by an unseen helper. You grab onto their wrists in turn, and are surprised at how quickly and easily you are able to scramble up the side of the hole. You take a good look at your rescuer—who do you see?

Perhaps you see the courageous part of yourself—the part that has already been courageous many times in the past and will be courageous many times in the future. Perhaps you see an image of God, or a divine force—an omnipresent, all-knowing, infinitely loving and supportive power that is always willing and able to help. Or perhaps you see another person in your life, and their own courage.

When you face your next challenge or fall into your next hole, remember that face of courage. No matter what that face looked like, the embodiment of courage that you saw is always with you, available to help you climb out of your hole. But first you must have the courage to ask.

{ 8 } Starry Blessings—Be Courageous and Grateful

When we face chronically challenging situations at work and home, our emotional water tanks are drained. When things heat up, and we find ourselves angry or upset, there's no water in the tank to cool us down. We run the risk of burning up, or burning someone else.

Gratitude re-fills the tank. The act of being grateful opens a spigot and lets cool refreshing water to flow back in. Gratitude is to anger like water is to fire. If you invite gratitude in, the flames of anger can no longer exist.

Imagine that you are at home and start having an argument with a loved one. As you feel your temperature rising, you realize you're not thinking clearly: your tanks are empty. You ask to be excused for a few minutes to clear your head and walk outside (without slamming the door, much as you'd like to). It's a crisp night, a refreshing relief from the heated, stuffy argument inside. As you walk, you can almost feel the anger radiating away from you, like heat waves off of blacktop. They radiate out into the night, and the sky's dark coolness begins to settle into you.

You know you need to refresh yourself and get back on Your To Be List. You remember gratitude as a way to refill your tank. You decide that for each star you see in the sky, you'll feel grateful for one thing in your life. You'll use the stars as an abacus to count your blessings.

"I'm grateful to get a break from the argument. I'm grateful for my house to keep me warm. I'm grateful that I have two feet to walk out here in the night air. I'm grateful for the night air..." You let your gratitude flow in a stream of consciousness, drawing grateful connections with everything you see and feel.

After a few minutes of counting your blessings, you feel yourself softening a little. Cooling off, getting some perspective. You're even ready to turn your attention and gratitude to the situation you just left. "I'm grateful that I'm still alive to argue. I'm grateful that we both have good minds and can both speak. I'm grateful that they're still alive. I'm grateful that they're not sick in the hospital. I'm grateful that this argument isn't all that serious in the grand scheme of things. I'm grateful that we both want to communicate about this and resolve it..."

When you're ready, you begin walking back, smiling at all the things you're grateful for. "I'm grateful for the beautiful fresh wildflowers by the side of the road. I'm grateful for the sidewalks that make it easy and safe for me to walk at night. I'm grateful for my shoes to protect my feet. I'm grateful that I can be refreshed by gratitude. I'm grateful for the door to my house, and for all the people who live inside..." You take a deep breath, smile, and enter with courage and gratitude.

{ 9 } Caring for the Future—Be Courageous and Bountiful

Sometimes we worry about the future. We imagine the future might be filled with scarcity and danger. We mistakenly believe that if we imagine what might go wrong in the future, we'll be safer. But worry never creates safety or bounty, or the courage to create them, either now or in the future.

Worry is visualizing, in great detail and with a powerful emotional fire, a future that we don't want. We must choose not to worry, but instead marshal our courage and look directly at our fears. If you have the habit of worrying about lack and scarcity, here's a path out: appreciate the abundance of the present moment.

First, come back to the here and now by giving your full attention to your breathing for three breaths.

Second, take three breaths, knowing that everything's okay right now. On your inhales, know: "I'm okay in this moment." On your exhales, know: "I have all the health [or money, or approval, or love] I need right now."

Finally, take three breaths, feeling the abundance within and around you right now. On your inhales: "I am so happy and grateful..." On your exhales: "...for the abundance of [fill in the blank] around me." You can think of your 50 trillion healthy cells, the air, the rays of sunshine, the multitude of raindrops, or the leaves on the trees.

In the past, you worried about scarcity in the future. But now that you're here, you can see that all that really matters is enjoying and appreciating the abundant wonders of the present moment. That will always be true.

The best thing you can do for your future is to practice appreciating the abundance in your present. Then, when you get to your future, you'll be better able to enjoy it.

{ 10 } Turning It Off—Be Courageous and Healing

The news is full of horror. Sometimes the news inspires us to take action. But sometimes it just makes us afraid, and the best thing to do to heal both ourselves and the situation is to turn it off.

We must be aware of what we're consuming through our eyes and ears, and make sure it's not feeding our fears. If we realize that the news is feeding our fears, we must turn it off. If it doesn't inspire us to take healing action right now, we must be courageous and change the channel.

News rushes at us like water from a fire hose. It doesn't quench our thirst, it just knocks us over. Businesses work very hard to get and keep our attention so that they can resell it to their advertisers. This is not a nefarious plot, it's just a business model. However, it is not our responsibility to give our attention to everything that's on the news. Rather, it is our responsibility to attend to, and heal, the suffering that is within us and around us.

We must be aware of the suffering in the world so that we can help transform it. We must take the outrage that we feel upon hearing about the brokenness, and channel that energy at once into Being Courageous, so that we can get busy with our repair work.

It's not irresponsible to turn off the news when it's feeding your fears. It's not weak to let the news take care of itself while you take care of yourself. It's not selfish to build your courage by focusing on the positive, beautiful, refreshing aspects of life. On the contrary, it's the most important thing you can do for the world.

May you courageously accept the responsibility of choosing To Be Healing.

8

Be Grateful—The Power to Receive

The universe is always giving to us. Twenty-
four hours a day. Seven days a week.

The universe supports and sustains us. It
gives us air to breathe. It gives us food to eat.
It gives us eyes to see and wonders to behold. It
gives us a heart to feel and people to love. The
universe abounds with miracles. If we have the
willingness to see these miracles, we can accept
them for the gifts that they truly are.

Sometimes what the universe offers us is so
simple and elemental that it becomes virtually
invisible to us. Take, for example, your breath.
When you were born, the first thing you did was to draw a breath. And
then you went on breathing, all day, every day, whether you were awake or
asleep, working or playing, silent or speaking. But if you pause to consider
everything your breath does for you and you will see it as the miracle it is:
Your breath infuses your body with life. Without breath, you could not feel,
think, say, or do anything. Your breath does so much for you—and you
never even have to ask for its support!

We are so fortunate to have the gift of breath, but we rarely think about
it. It is the simplest element of our lives, yet we rarely feel grateful for our
breath. In fact, because we have breath, we are receiving something mirac-

RELATED TO BE'S
Be Thankful
Be Appreciative
Be Prayerful
Be Sincere
Be Yielding
Be Reverent
Be Reflective
Be Releasing

ulous from the universe every moment we are alive. Because of our breath, we always have something to feel grateful for, every moment of the day.

And that is just the start of what we have to be grateful for. If you are looking this book, it is because you are experiencing the gift of sight. If you are reading these words it is because of the remarkable ability of the human brain to turn abstract symbols into language. Sight is a miracle. So is reading.

We have so much to be grateful for if we have the eyes to see and the heart to receive. And once we begin to find reasons to be grateful we will see more and more.

There are times in our lives that we feel that we have nothing to be grateful for. When we feel this way, it is because we are looking at the world backwards: We want the big things life has to offer first. We want our dream house, or the perfect relationship, or a day that is free of troubles. And we imagine that once we are sitting in our dream house, looking out at a sunset with the love of our lives at the end of a trouble-free day, we will finally be able to lean back and feel grateful for all the simple things in life. But we really must begin by receiving the smallest, simplest gifts with gratitude, because it is from these simple gifts that the larger gifts ultimately flow.

Imagine a child who is given a small token of a friends' affection: a favorite baseball card or a well-worn and much-beloved stuffed animal. The child who receives the gift, who had hoped for something larger and more expensive, tosses the gift aside, petulantly crosses his arms, and refuses to say "Thank you." Do you think the friend will want to give the ungrateful child another larger treasure in the future? And even if the friend did give the ungrateful child another, larger gift in the future, do you think that the ungrateful child will know how to say "thank you" with sincerity if he did not practice saying thank you with the smaller gift? The child has made some profound errors.

When we choose To Be Grateful, we will learn to say "thank you" to the world for the small gifts it offers us: our breath, our eyes, our heart, the shining sun, a beautiful flower, the friendships we enjoy, and the love we are able to feel for others. And the more we choose To Be Grateful, the more that we will see that these are not small gifts at all, but gifts of profound meaning and infinite magnitude. And just like the child who learns to say thank you for the humble and heartfelt gift, we will find that our hearts will be open and ready to receive.

There were times throughout our adoption process that the two of us felt overwhelmed by the challenges the universe threw our way. But challenges are in themselves a kind of gift. And through these challenges we came to know on an even deeper level the value of family and friendship. We came to see that we had family and friends on the other side of the world. By staying rooted in gratitude, we were able to see that standing just behind every challenge was a gift waiting to be offered.

Choosing To Be Grateful means choosing to receive what the universe offers with joyous thanksgiving.

The 10 How's

{ 1 } The Cage of Desire—Be Grateful and Free

Gratitude is the opposite of desire. When we are grateful for what is real, here and now, we are free from desire. When we are focused on what we have, it is impossible to also focus on what we lack.

The goal of this exercise is not to eliminate your desires, but to release the burden they impose on you. It's only by releasing your desire that the desire can release you.

Think of one of your desires that feel particularly painful or burdensome to you. For example, the desire to make more money, or lose ten pounds, or attract a soulmate. Imagine that the object of your desire is in a cage, with bars just wide enough for you to reach your hand through. But when you reach in and grab it, you find that the slats are not wide enough for you to get your fist back out! You are trapped with your fist gripped tightly around your desire.

Now imagine that all the things you actually have (your current salary, your current health, your current relationships) are on the other side of the room. Your choice is clear: stay here with your hand trapped in the cage of your desire, or release your grip and gratefully embrace what you already have.

Very slowly, feel your grip releasing. Feel the liberation spreading over you as your hand slips out of the bars. You are free to walk across the room to your real life, waiting patiently on the other side.

{ 2 } Precious Gifts—Be Grateful and Happy

Every moment is a gift. It's an offer of happiness from the Universe to you. The Universe has spent countless eons delicately handcrafting this moment, wrapping it in limitless splendor, and preparing to gently present it to you. How would you like to receive it? With entitlement or with gratitude?

Imagine an enormous hand reaching down and handing you a beautiful gift. Open the card—what does the Universe have to say to you? Imagine the boundlessly kind and encouraging words written inside. You can look at this card whenever you need to remember how much the Universe loves you.

While you're unwrapping the gift, take note of the delightful designs on the paper. Now slowly and deliberately lift up the gift for all to see. What has the Universe given you? It's the gift of this moment! There is no greater gift than this moment—the gift that allows you to enjoy all of the Universe's other gifts.

You can say to yourself, "I am so happy and grateful to receive the gift of this moment."

{ 3 } The Settling Lake—Be Grateful and Peaceful

A tremendous peace of mind comes with being grateful. It's like a "Buy One Get One Free" offer: Be Grateful, and get Peaceful free! The act of giving thanks for all you have right now signals your mind that all is well, and makes you feel peaceful.

Imagine a lake that has been stirred up by a passing rainstorm. The surface is choppy, the depths are turbulent, and the water is clouded with silt. Imagine sitting by the side of the lake and being grateful for the blessings in your life.

You smile and say, "Thank you for the blessing of my family. I am grateful for all their strengths and virtues. And I am even grateful for all their craziness, which keeps me challenged and keeps life interesting. Thank you for the blessing of my family." As you feel this gratitude for your family, the surface of the water begins to quiet.

You smile and say, "Thank you for the blessing of my health. I am grateful for all the vitality, strength, and ease that I have right now—and for all the aches and pains that I don't have right now. I am even grateful for the aches and pains I do have, large and small. I know that they are simply part of my experience right now. Thank you for the blessing of my health." As you feel this gratitude, the inner turbulence of the lake calms and stills.

You smile and say, "Thank you for the blessing of my work. I am grateful for the creativity, self-expression, stability, personal growth and prosperity it gives me right now. I am even grateful for all the annoying, dysfunctional, exhausting and stifling parts, as they show me what needs to change, either in myself or in the organization. Thank you for the blessing of my work." As you feel this gratitude, the silt begins to settle.

Continue being grateful for the many blessings in your life, and watch the water become still, calm, clear, peaceful. The more you practice this gratitude exercise, the more peaceful your mind will become.

{ 4 } The Faithful Friend—Be Grateful and Loving

Imagine you have a very special friend—the kind that only comes around once in several lifetimes. This friend was there with you from the very instant of your birth, and grew with you through the years—from baby to child to teen to this very moment.

She gleefully raced up and down hills with you, grieved lost love with you, kept all your innermost secrets. Your friend knows when you are hurt or lonely, jubilant or reverent, and has complete understanding and compassion for you. You know that your friend will stay with you and support you every single day for the rest of your life.

This faithful friend is your heart.

Put your hand over your heart now and feel its steady beat. Smile and send your love to your heart. Feel grateful and happy that you have such a friend with whom to share and sustain your life.

{ 5 } Eyesight Day—Be Grateful and Strong

How much of your life are you taking for granted: your friends, your family, your home, your mind, your abilities to walk, talk, see, and hear? We all take things for granted—it's the easiest thing in the world to do. It takes strength to choose to be grateful.

Pick one miraculous gift that you know you're taking for granted, and celebrate it all day today. For example, declare today "Eyesight Day," and decide that you're going to be grateful for your eyesight, as many times as you can, for the rest of the day.

Say to yourself, "I am so happy and grateful for my eyesight right now." Declare your gratitude for your eyesight when you are driving in your car, when you're at the cafeteria, when you're using your computer, when you're talking with people at work, when you see your friends and loved ones. Use all your strength of focus to keep your gratitude front and center all day.

How many times can you make that declaration of gratitude? Ten, fifty, a hundred? What if you put yourself into a momentary state of gratitude a hundred times in a day? How would that change your day?

{ 6 } The Best GPS—Be Grateful and Balanced

Our intuition will guide us back to balance every time—if we listen. How marvelous is that? It's like a GPS that always shows us the way back home to ourselves. The more we can catch it in action and give thanks for it, the more powerful it will become.

Stand on one leg for a moment and let yourself wobble. Every time you go off balance, just get back on. In the moment of correcting your balance, give thanks to all of your internal balancing systems. Do this a few times, becoming conscious of how exquisite it is that your body knows just what to do to keep you balanced.

Now look at your life, and remember a moment recently when you got off balance and then back on. Maybe you got angry at your kids, but then cooled down. Maybe you were being a workaholic, and took a break to get reacquainted with the rest of your life. In each case, your intuition told you exactly what you needed to do to get back in balance. Feel thankful for the gift of your intuition, and for the gift of balance in your life.

{ 7 } Gratitude Sprints—Be Grateful and Courageous

Time yourself for ten minutes. As fast as you can, think of everything you can possibly think of to be grateful for. Phrase each as a sentence, starting with, "I'm grateful for..."

Keep going for the whole ten minutes. The first few minutes will be easy, but then you may find it getting strenuous. Stick with it, and keep going as fast as you can, even if you can only think of seemingly minor things like, "I'm grateful for the chair I'm sitting in."

When you're running sprints, the last few yards, when your lungs are gasping for air, are where you really build your endurance. When you're lifting weights, the last few reps, when your limbs are shaking, are the ones that challenge the muscles to grow stronger. When you're doing grati-tude sprints, the last few minutes, when you're really reaching for some-thing to be grateful for, are the ones that build lasting power in your grati-tude muscles.

You can do Gratitude Sprints anywhere—standing in line at the gro-cery store, stuck in traffic, walking briskly to your next meeting. Decide that between now and the time you get to the cash register, or the next intersection, or the meeting, you'll be grateful for absolutely everything you see, hear, smell, think and feel. If you're in line it might be, "I'm so grateful for chewing gum, for *Prevention* magazine, for all the food in my cart, for the money I'll use to pay, for the person standing in front of me..."

You'll notice immediate results from doing Gratitude Sprints—your life will magically be filled with amazing gifts that were there all along.

{ 8 } Gratitude Deep Dive—Be Grateful

Think of one person or event in your life for which you are extremely grateful. Perhaps it's a memory of a special time with a grandparent or a friend. Perhaps it's an opportunity that came along at just the right time and changed your life. Perhaps it's a person who has always been there for you, through thick and thin.

Hold your special person or event in your mind and join your palms at your heart. Imagine yourself on the end of a diving board, and raise your hands from your heart over your head. Picture yourself diving into a pool of gratitude for everything that brought your special person or event into your life. As you dive deeper into the pool, you become more deeply grateful.

At the top of the pool, you are at the level of Appreciation: You recognize what you like in this person or event. You fully understand the meaning or importance the special person or event has in your life.

As you plunge deeper you are Thankful: You thank the source of your special person or event. You thank God, thank the Universe, thank serendipity. Say thank you to everything that was in the right place at the right time to make your special person or event possible.

Finally, you arrive at the level of Reverence: You feel a sense of profound respect and awe for your special person or event, and for all that allowed it to be. Stay with this reverence for a few moments, in a very deep and quiet place, before swimming back up.

{ 9 } Sharing The Earth—Be Grateful and Bountiful

Think of all the people you love and who love you—and know that at this very moment they are walking on the same ground and breathing the same air. Feel your feet touch the same earth that supports them. Breathe that sweet air that sustains them.

At every moment your gratitude has the capacity to connect you with everyone you love, even when they are not present. Breathing this way, walking on the earth this way, you are engaged with the miracle of the great bounty of love. There is a new fullness in each breath. A deep meaning in each step. What a bountiful gift it is to be able to breathe and walk with gratitude.

{ 10 } Thanking The Past—Be Grateful and Healing

We all know that the past is gone—there's no changing it. But yet it binds us, constricts us, burdens us. While we can't change the past, we can heal it. We can use the elixir of gratitude to heal the past with this exercise. In this exercise, we will free the past by thanking it, sincerely and completely, for bringing us to right now.

Join your palms, as in prayer, and say thank you to this morning. "Dear morning, I am so grateful to you. Some things went the way I wanted, and some didn't. But no matter what happened, dear morning, without you I know that I wouldn't be here right now, I wouldn't be exactly who I am. Thank you, morning—you can go now." You may want to do a little bow, and some sort of "freeing" motion, as if you were releasing a bird into the air, or a leaf into a stream.

Now thank yesterday, in the same way. You can thank last week, last year. Thank the wonderful, happy times, for they have shaped you and brought you to this moment. Thank the difficult and unhappy times, for they have shaped you and brought you to this moment.

How far back into the past would you like to thank? The moments leading up to your birth? All the moments in the lives of your grandparents, that were required to take place in order for you to be born? All the way back to the dinosaurs? Thank and release it all!

May your gratitude heal your past, and in so doing, heal your present, and many generations into the future.

9

Be Bountiful—The Power to Give

We give so much of ourselves to the world each and every day. We love, we nurture, we support, and we encourage. We offer help, we collaborate, and we create. We listen, we offer wisdom, and we provide comfort. We give and we give and we give of ourselves. We are giving because we have a generous spirit. We are giving because it is the right thing to do. We are giving because we know of no other way we would want to be.

RELATED TO BE'S

Be Prosperous

Be Abundant

Be Generous

Be Successful

Be Flourishing

Be Intentional

Be Blessed

And yet there are times we feel that we have given too much of ourselves away. We feel that we are wearing down. We are exhausted. We feel invisible to the people who should appreciate us most. And we fear that if we give one thing more, we might dry up and vanish altogether.

In our private moments we wonder how we can go on giving if we do not receive in return.

So we learn to hold ourselves back. We become misers of our inner treasure. We ration our feelings and withhold our vision. We refuse to offer the world the gift of who we truly are because we fear that what is truly valuable within us might be taken away from us and heedlessly squandered by people who neither understand nor appreciate us. We worry that someone might take what is precious from us and we will never find it within our hearts again.

Imagine a child bouncing a new ball on the playground. She is enjoying playing with the ball and feeling very lucky to have it. Then the ball rolls away and just as she is running to retrieve it, a group of children—unaware that the ball belonged to the girl—run up and grab the ball before she can reach it. As they run off, the little girl bursts into tears. She is miserable. She has the impression that, not only have the children taken her ball, they have also taken her happiness. But that could only be possible if the happiness were in the ball. How could that be? Is happiness so small that it could be squeezed into a small rubber sphere?

Of course not.

Happiness is an energy that is infinite. If we were to comfort this child, we would dry her tears and ask her to look around and see that there are countless reasons to be happy. We would show her that the sun was shining and the air was fresh. We would remind her of the swings and slides on the playground. We would tell her that there was still fun to be had and friends to be made. And then she would smile and run off to play, having the sense that her happiness has returned. But in truth it was never gone. Happiness was always within her, an infinite bounty waiting to be revealed.

We also have within us an infinite bounty waiting to be revealed. *We will never run out of what we did not create in the first place.* We can never run out of the energies on our To Be List. Those energies are always available.

It may be that, like the little girl in the story, we need time to refresh ourselves and find that energy within us once again. But with support and with practice, we will learn to access the bountiful treasure within us with confidence and ease.

Each of us is a gift to the world: a unique revelation of Infinite Light. Each of us is an open channel through which universal energies flow without end. We are, by nature, recipients and givers of these energies. When we see this fact, we will feel free to give of ourselves, for we know that what we offer with the wisdom of this understanding will be replenished within us. So we should offer our light to the world with gratitude, just as we receive in gratitude, because where there is true bounty, every act of giving becomes an act of receiving. And every act of receiving is an act of giving.

Recently, our friends Kimra and Spud came to visit and we began reminiscing about the day we returned from Kazakhstan. We recalled the balloons on the mailboxes, the neighbors who came out to greet us, and the banner and the yellow ribbons that awaited us at our home. We all became very emotional when we began to recall what that day meant to us. We told our friends how grateful we still were for their selfless acts of kindness and support and how we could never truly repay them for what they did for us.

Kimra shook her head. "No," she said, "It's *us* who should thank *you.* The opportunity to help you and your family was a gift to us. It expanded our world. It expanded our hearts. It made us feel that anyone in the world could be our family. It changed who we were and helped us to grow in ways we never imagined."

We thought we were the recipients of the great bounty of love and friendship. It turned out that we were givers of bounty by sharing our vision and our hearts with our friends.

So, choose To Be Bountiful. Offer the world the bounty of your heart. And trust that by giving, you will receive.

The 10 How's

{ 1 } I Have Enough—Be Bountiful and Free

When we get into "scarcity thinking" mode, we don't feel free at all. We feel bound and constricted. Scarcity is just an idea—usually a worry about an imagined future—and when we chain ourselves to this notion that there will never be enough, we lose our freedom.

We envision some future time when we might not have enough. We worry that we might not have enough money, enough love, enough health, as if the worry could inoculate us against scarcity. But the worry actually tethers us to the idea of scarcity.

Freedom comes with knowing the truth that in this very moment, you have enough. You have everything you need to survive. This is self-evident:

you're alive right now, so you must have everything you need right now to stay alive. This has been true every moment until now, or you wouldn't be here. It will continue to be true for every single future moment of your life. As long as you live, you will always have everything you need to exist.

We all have desires—we want more love, more money, more health. But it's vital to our freedom that we separate desire from requirement, as this is the dividing line between survival and meaning. If we mistakenly believe that we don't have enough to survive, our fight-or-flight system goes on high alert, and we are not free at all. But if we take ourselves out of survival mode by knowing we have enough right this moment, we are free to enter into the realm of creating meaning.

The practice is to simply acknowledge the truth of bounty—feeling it in your bones. "Right now, I have all the love I need. In this very moment, I have all the money I need. Right now, I have all the health I need." When you really feel the feeling deep inside you of having enough, you are set free.

{ 2 } Tea Ceremony—Be Bountiful and Happy

"One is rich who is happy with their lot." The way to be happy is to be happy with what you have. The way to be rich is to be happy with what you have. This exercise is to practice being happy with the simple things in life, like a cup of tea.

Imagine you have made yourself a cup of tea, and are sitting quietly. Look around you and smile at what you see. Alternate between appreciating all the bounty surrounding you and taking a ceremonial sip of tea. Each sip of tea should be slow, regal, and deliberate. Give each sip your full attention.

Start with the tea itself, "I'm so happy I have this nice warm tea in my hands." Sip the tea slowly and happily.

"I'm so happy that I have hands which can feel the warmth of the teacup—it's so comforting, and brings back delightful memories." A ceremonial sip of tea.

"I'm so happy that I have this chair to sit on, and a good strong back which allows me to sit in comfort and ease." A happy, luxurious sip of tea.

Keep it up for at least 10 appreciative sips of tea, or until you feel very happy with the bounty that surrounds you.

{ 3 } Peaceful Snowflakes—Be Bountiful and Peaceful

When you feel the feelings of having more than enough, your mind and body are signaled to relax and feel peaceful. Tuning into the bounty all around you is a sure way to grow the peace in your life.

Imagine that it's nighttime on one of the shortest, coldest, darkest days of the year. You're out in the country, and step outside for a breath of fresh air. You look up and notice that it has started snowing. The snow-flakes are huge and soft, filling the sky. Everywhere you look there are snowflakes. You notice the intense hush, and within the stillness you can hear the individual flakes delicately landing. Time is suspended in mid-air, and you vow to carry this moment forward with you as a shining example of being bountiful and peaceful.

You can also practice feeling the peaceful bounty of the stars in the sky, the dirt on the ground, the leaves on the trees, the wind in the grass, or even the winking taillights of traffic on a highway. When you slow down into the present moment, you can notice the peaceful bounty all around.

{ 4 } The Sack of Pebbles—Be Bountiful and Loving

When we feel bountiful, we are free to give with love. If we feel as though we're fighting for our very existence, there's no space for love. But if we're rolling in plenty, it's very natural to give our attention, and our loving com-passion, to others.

Imagine that you are standing on a main street in your town or neigh-borhood. You have beside you a sack of pebbles. Whenever someone passes you, they stop, curious about your sack. You look deeply into their eyes, and then select a pebble that is just perfect for them at that moment. If they need healing, you select a healing pebble. If they need joy, you select a joyful pebble. If they need peace, you select a peaceful pebble. You smile gently as you press the pebble into their palm and watch as they realize it's just what they needed.

You can do this in real life, too, but without the pebbles. You are abundant with gifts to be given. You have the power to give your friends and loved ones just what they need. The more you give away "pebbles" of joy, peace, and healing, the more you'll realize you still have in your sack.

{ 5 } The Wildflower in the Parking Lot—Be Bountiful and Strong

Have you ever seen a wildflower growing up through the pavement? The life force in its tiny seed is so strong and plentiful that it can crack asphalt. The little flower is a triumph of life over lifelessness and beauty over monotony.

The same force that propels the seedling through the sidewalk also powers all the life on our planet. It's the same magical force that causes cells to subdivide and grow, that draws sap improbably a hundred feet up a sequoia trunk, that organizes several dozen pounds of carbon, hydrogen and oxygen into a human being. Whether we call it life force, or the Universe, or God's will, it is incomprehensibly abundant, and indescribably mighty.

Imagine that you are a wildflower seed, lying dormant beneath a corner of a parking lot. An unseen yet unmistakable wave of energy engulfs you and signals that the time has come to awaken. You know just what to do, and begin the journey. When your head brushes up against the bottom of the pavement, you send out a call for strength. You feel the life force rushing in to support you: water and minerals expanding your cells, roots and ground providing a solid footing for you to push against.

Just as you're about to give up, you feel the pavement crack above your head. A sliver of bright light opens up. You quickly grow into the daylight, preparing to share your unique bloom with the world around you.

Which seeds inside you are ready to crack the pavement of your old habits and patterns? Feel the life force rushing in, bountiful and strong, signaling those seeds that it's time to begin the journey to their full potential.

{ 6 } The Intuitive Force Field—Be Bountiful and Balanced

As we make our way through our days, we encounter bountiful blessings—from the kindness of others to the beauty of nature. We also encounter an abundance of that which is not so wonderful—everything from gossip at the water cooler, to foods that we know are not healthy for us. For better and for worse, our environment is bountiful in every way.

Our job is to interact with our bountiful environment in a way that keeps us balanced.

Imagine you have an invisible outer skin, like a protective force field that completely surrounds you. This force field only lets through precisely what you need to stay balanced. If a negative influence comes into contact with it, it lights up, to let you know that this is not right for you at the moment, and the force field becomes impenetrable.

Imagine you're at the metaphorical water cooler, and the colleague you're chitchatting with begins to gossip. See the force field around you lighting up and repelling the unwanted influence, as if the words were bouncing off your outer skin. See yourself easily and firmly changing the subject.

Imagine it's the end of the day, and you're tired, and the cookies in the cookie jar are screaming your name. Just as you reach out to grab one, your force field lights up. See yourself easily and deliberately grab a glass of water instead and leave the kitchen to read a good book.

In real life, your intuition is the force field. It lights up with a warning signal when you encounter a choice that is out of alignment with your true values, the real meaning in your life. If you want To Be Loving, gossip won't do it. If you want to Be Healing, unhealthy food is not the right choice.

Listen to your intuition, and it will tell you how to interact with the bountiful environment, letting in only the bounty that is balancing for you.

{ 7 } You, the Multi-Millionaire—Be Bountiful and Courageous

Why isn't it easier to count our blessings? Because we're afraid of losing them. We think: Better not to have loved and lost.

This is a common block to feeling truly bountiful and abundant. We have the notion that if we really appreciate what we have, and then lose it, the pain will be more intense. To Be Bountiful, we must courageously face the fear of loss.

This exercise asks you to imagine the value of all the things in your life: your body, your mind, your loved ones, etc. This can be scary, because it implies that those things might go away. The reality is that everything changes, and everything in our lives will be transformed at some time in the future. To feel the rich bounty in our lives, we must to have the courage to appreciate what we have right now, even though we are certain to lose it all eventually. You can't take it with you, and the more deeply you accept that, the more profound will be your appreciation of the abundance that's here now.

Add up how much your life is worth to you right now. Bust out a calculator, or a pencil, or a spreadsheet (if you're one of those kinds of people), and get to adding.

How much would you pay for your eyes? Force yourself to write down a number, even if it's far more than you have in your checking account, and it most likely is.

Now, add the value of your ears. If for some reason, God forbid, you were to no longer have properly functioning ears, what would you pay to get them back?

Add in values of your right hand, your left hand, your two arms, your feet, your legs, your skull, your brain, your nose, your lips, your tongue, your teeth, your hair, your skin, your spine, your heart, your lungs, your stomach, your kidneys, your liver, and your bones. Add in the value of your mind, your ability to talk, your ability to walk, your ability to reason, your creativity. Feeling wealthy yet?

But wait, there's more! How much would you pay for your best friend? How about your mother? Your child? Father, sisters, brothers, children, other relatives. Now, add in what you'd pay for your fondest memories.

And the grand total is? Astronomical. Turns out, you can't afford you! You have a multi-million dollar life taking place all around you at this very moment. Even if you own a house and a car, their resale values pale in comparison to the sum you've just computed. Jot down the total on a scrap of paper, and tuck it in your wallet. That's your real net worth.

It can be scary to confront the value of all you have. But if you approach this exercise with a spirit of courage and bounty, you will see how truly rich you are.

{ 8 } Everyday Thanksgiving—Be Bountiful and Grateful

In the U.S., the holiday of Thanksgiving celebrates the bounty that the Europeans and Native Americans shared at the end of the Europeans' first harvest season. Modern Americans have a special feeling about Thanksgiving, as it's a rare moment of culturally sanctioned gratitude for all the plenty that we have.

Imagine yourself at the original Thanksgiving table. Last winter was the roughest one you've ever faced, and many of your friends and family approached the doorway of starvation as supplies ran perilously low. The community worked dawn to dusk all through the growing season, and it looks as if your efforts have paid off. You have brought in enough of the harvest to assure your survival through the coming winter.

Feel your gratitude for the sweet potatoes, for the squash, and for the corn. You have taken care of them all summer as they converted the nutrition of the soil and sunlight into nutrition that you can use. Feel your gratitude for the deer whose life your hunters have taken to sustain the community. Know that through the bounty of these plants and animals, your continued existence is ensured. You silently say a prayer of gratitude, thanking the Creator for providing this blessing.

In your daily life, you can bring this Thanksgiving energy to every meal. It was true for the first celebration, and it's true for every meal we eat: by the grace of God, we have more than enough. No matter what time of year it is, resolve to make your next meal a Thanksgiving meal.

{ 9 } The Zucchini Method—Be Bountiful

The essence of Plenty is zucchini. Is anyone ever low on zucchini? Whenever you plant it, you always get enough to share with all your neighbors.

Not only is the squash an example of a bountiful harvest, it also points us to a powerful way to manifest bounty in our lives.

When you plant a zucchini seed, you know without a doubt that if you give it enough water, it will grow into a zucchini plant and provide plentiful squash. You know for a fact that your seed is intended to grow into a zucchini plant, and it that will fulfill the intention.

When you want to manifest a particular sort of bounty in your life—whether it be plentiful money, profound love, or vibrant health—use the Zucchini Method:

1) *Plant the seed of crystal-clear intention.*

Phrase your intention with positive, personal, present tense. The intention should be one of Natural Plenty—not so big that it's unnatural, and not so small that it's not Bountiful. Think zucchinis: natural plenty.

2) *Expect natural bounty.*

Be the way you wish to be, as if your desire has already come to pass. Think those thoughts, feel those feelings, and do those actions. Put these To Be's on Your To Be List: Be Free, Be Happy, Be Peaceful, etc.

3) *Water the seedling every day.*

Water your intention with the feelings of the desired states. Use Your To Be List to remind you to return to the way you want To Be over and over again. The seed of your intention will only grow when watered with the positive states of being on Your To Be List.

Let go of any worries that it might not turn out the way you want it. You have planted a zucchini seed—it will grow into a zucchini. You don't know exactly how the zucchini will grow, exactly which lumps and bumps it will have when you harvest it, but you know that it will grow into a zucchini. If you plant a seed of love and water it with loving thoughts, feelings and actions, it will grow into love. If you plant a seed of wealth and water it with wealthy thoughts, feelings and actions, it will grow into wealth.

The best thing about using the Zucchini Method of manifestation is that when you practice feeling exactly the way you want to feel when you have achieved your desire, then in the most important sense, you have already achieved it. You're done. You are no longer focusing on your shadow goals, but on your real goals, all of which start with the word "Be."

There are no worries, there is no striving, there is no struggle. You don't worry that your zucchini seed might grow into poison ivy. The zucchini doesn't strive to grow. You do not struggle to make it grow faster or slower or different. You just let it peacefully unfold into its Natural Plenty.

The Zucchini Method is stress-free, enjoyable, and easy. It's also the only way that really works to get you what you really want.

{ 10 } The Healing Superstore—Be Bountiful and Healing

When you practice being bountiful, it keeps you out of survival mode and in meaning mode. In survival mode, you physically can't heal. Biological research shows that when the human system is activated to cope with an external threat, it diverts all the energy from dealing with internal threats, i.e. healing. It's a wise move to focus on survival before healing—first get away from the saber-toothed tiger, then deal with your sniffles. We have to move ourselves out of survival mode in order to heal, and a wonderful way to get out of survival mode is to practice being bountiful.

Imagine yourself entering a gigantic healing superstore. In the cavernous store you can find every kind of healing, all in massive quantities. Whatever kind of healing is needed for any problem—from a sprained ankle to a strained relationship, from intense anger to existential angst—all the solutions are in the superstore. Forgiveness Flakes is in Aisle Four, Happiness Helper in Aisle Six, and Creativity Cola is on special this week. All of these products exist in abundance in the store.

You walk into the store, looking for just the right healing for yourself right now. Let your intuition guide you to just the right aisle, just the right shelf, just the right package. What do you need right now—to be forgiving, to be joyful, to strengthen your boundaries, to relax your boundaries? When you have found just the right package of healing, take it from the shelf and feel it magically working. Feel the healing product spreading over you with its miraculous curative effects.

Though this visualization is purely fantasy, it primes the mind for something much bigger. We all want abundance, but why? To what end? We know we can't take it with us.

The meaning of bounty is healing. We must use the bounty in our lives to heal ourselves and those around us. Healing gives meaning to our desires for abundance.

First get out of survival mode and know the reality that you have enough right now. Then let your intuition guide you to just the right healing for yourself. Only then will you be the most effective healer you can be for yourself and the people around you.

May you see and appreciate the bounty all around you, so you can give of yourself to repair the brokenness in our world.

10

Be Healing—The Power to Change Your World

We barely have to roll out of bed in the morning to be confronted with the fact that the world is in tatters. The clock radio, set to the morning news, wakes us from our dreams with a sudden jolt that reminds us the world is at war. Ethnic minorities are ravaged by oppression. Local communities are torn apart by violence and poverty. In our own families, arguments both frivolous and grave chip away at our sense of safety and comfort. And deep within our hearts, there are places that are torn asunder, broken, or even shattered.

RELATED TO BE'S

Be Whole

Be Holistic

Be Holy

Be Complete

Be Awake

Be Restoring

Be Rejuvenating

Be Transformational

Be A Blessing

Be Yourself

Unfortunately, this seems to be a typical state of affairs. History shows us that civilizations have always been at war. Sociologists maintain that minorities have always been oppressed. Family therapists will testify to the fact that the seeds of discord are inherent within the family structure itself. And the woes of the human heart have been well documented by poets for millennia.

So, given that conflict seems the rule and not the exception, why should we expect anything different from our world, from our community, from our families, or from ourselves? If conflict and the suffering that arises from it are the status quo of human existence, why are we not used to it by now?

The truth is we are not used to conflict. Every ounce of our being cries out against it. In fact, the language we use to describe these inner and outer conflicts indicates that something in our world has gone desperately awry. If we say that our world is "ravaged," "broken," "torn asunder," and "shattered" by conflict and heartache—then we are indicating that the natural order of the world is to be peaceful and whole. We intuitively feel that there is a state of existence that is more essential than the world that we experience every day. And that essential state is Oneness.

The Jewish mystical tradition of Kabbalah uses a story to explain how our world, once whole, was first shattered. It says that when the world was first created, the Source of the World attempted to fill the world with Infinite Divine Light. But because the creation was not strong enough to contain that powerful, primordial light, it was shattered into pieces. Yet every shard contained within it some remnant of that original Divine Light. So now, the Divine Light is hidden. Every human, plant, animal, and object contains a spark of that Divine Light.

But the story goes on to explain that we humans have a profound role in healing the world and bringing it back to a state of wholeness.

Our job, while we are living and breathing on this earth, is to repair the world and restore it to its original state of wholeness. We do this by seeing the Divine Spark within every living being and inanimate object. When we see the sacred shining within the mundane, we liberate the spark that was imprisoned within it, thus returning it to its Divine Source. The mundane becomes sacred as its inner light shines and illuminates the world around it.

This imagery touches something deep within us if we have the sense that there is a sacred and shining wholeness standing just behind the fractured world we witness with our eyes, hear with our ears, and touch with our hands. Behind everything that is broken—in the world, in our communities, in our relationships, and in our own hearts—there is something crying out to be made whole.

So when we hear that cry, we must respond to the sacred that is hidden within the mundane. We are saying to the sacred light within: "I hear you. I know you are there. I am here to help."

When we respond to the world as sacred, we are choosing To Be Healing.

Choosing To Be Healing requires that you use the energies on Your To Be List to release the hidden light within everything you encounter.

- *Choosing To Be Free* releases the light of vision.
- *Choosing To Be Happy* releases the light of joy.
- *Choosing To Be Peaceful* releases the light of peace.
- *Choosing To Be Loving* releases the light of compassion.
- *Choosing To Be Strong* releases the light of inner power.
- *Choosing To Be Balanced* releases the light of equanimity.
- *Choosing To Be Courageous* releases the light of thoughtful action.
- *Choosing To Be Grateful* releases the light of appreciation.
- *Choosing To Be Bountiful* releases the light of infinite possibility.

So we must open ourselves and share the light that dwells within us: our joy, our inner peace, our compassion, our power, our balance, our thoughtfulness, our appreciation, and the bounty of infinite possibility. And we do this not just because it will improve our lives (which it will!), but because it is healing to a world so much in need of healing.

We can heal with a smile. We can heal with a kind word. We can heal with creativity. We can heal by taking action. Or we can heal by sitting quietly in gratitude. We can heal alone. Or we can heal with community. There are infinite ways To Be Healing in this world. But it all begins with seeing the world for what it truly is: sacred and shining with inner light.

Mother Teresa once said: "If we have no peace, it is because we have forgotten that we belong to each other." Peace—in the world and within ourselves—begins with remembrance. This is not a memory of a historical fact, but a deeper memory that lies within our hearts. It is a memory that is contained within that sacred spark in each of us. The roots of the word "remember" mean "to put together again." When we remember that we belong to one another, we are not only recalling a deep spiritual truth of our existence, we are bringing the world back to wholeness through healing.

Our family's decision to adopt two children from the other side of the world not only made our family whole, it brought a community together for a common purpose, and helped people see that even in the wake of unconscionable acts of violence, meaning can emerge, hearts can come together, and the light of the sacred can shine. The two of us did not make this happen alone. We simply chose to be parents to two beautiful children in need, and the hearts of our neighbors opened and the healing light from their hearts surrounded us. And it was in the healing light of their hearts that we began our lives as a family together. That light shines all around our family to this day.

The choice To Be Healing is a choice to be who you truly are: a shining light that brings wholeness to the world.

The 10 How's

{ 1 } The Birdcage—Be Healing and Free

What are you holding onto that you know needs to be released? Is it lack of forgiveness, childhood hurt, limiting beliefs, bodily tension, an unhealthy relationship? So long as you're gripping tightly to any of these negative patterns, your healing will impeded. Your vitality depends on letting them go, turning them loose, and becoming free.

Imagine there's a birdcage inside you. The bird that lives in the cage is the pattern you need to release. The bird can be unforgiveness, hurt, belief, relationship, or body tension. You can see that the bird desperately wants to be set free—he's banging around in there, making a lot of noise, trying to escape, trying to get your attention so you will let him out.

You look at the bird with your whole heart, and tell him, "I know you want to be free. I heard you making all that noise, and I'm sorry I didn't pay attention before. I'll let you go now." Then open the cage with love, and watch the bird scramble out of the cage and soar up into the blue sky. Your bird circles once, as if to say goodbye, and vanishes over the horizon.

The cage inside you has also vanished. Place your hands over your heart and smile, feeling light and bright, airy and free, like the bird you have released.

{ 2 } Giggle Rx—Be Healing and Happy

Even our most gripping problems lose their hold on us when we laugh. Laughter and vexation can't coexist. They're like fire and water—they can't occupy the same space. One burns, the other soothes.

But when we're mired in our troubles, often the last thing we feel like doing is putting on a happy face. It's one of life's great ongoing challenges to pull ourselves up by our bootstraps out of our troubles and into a happier mindset. Laughter is the perfect medicine, and sometimes it only takes a teaspoonful of giggles to crack open the channel to healing.

We laugh when we see an issue in a wider and wiser context. Our perspective is broadened. We zoom out and see more of the landscape, and suddenly the smaller picture to which we were clinging seems ridiculous. The healing happens because we release our attachment to the narrower view.

A trick for dissolving a problem is to move your mind back and forth between your problem and something that makes you laugh. First, decide on some image or memory or scene that always gives you a giggle. Maybe it's something hilarious your child said. Perhaps it's imagining your high school principal wearing a tutu. Possibly it's remembering your favorite Steve Martin or Will Farrell sketch, or the funniest line from a recent comedy movie.

Think about your problem for a moment. Just long enough to start feeling dragged down by it. Then switch to the scene that gives you a chuckle. Move back and forth a couple of times until you're able to smile at your problem. The problem may not have gone away, but you've lightened its burden, and released its grip on you a bit.

{ 3 } Cracking the Egg—Be Healing and Peaceful

Stillness is a powerful force. Don't be fooled by its passive demeanor. Stillness has the capacity to crack open our most calcified problems and allow healing to flow in.

Pick a problem that's been hanging around for too long. Imagine that it's encased in a hard, eggshell-like exterior. Imagine holding the egg of your problem in your hands while you become very still. Sit in such a way that you can let your body be still. Let your emotions become still for a moment. Release any tension or tightness in your mind, and let it become still, your thoughts settling down like leaves falling to the ground. Feel your spirit in your body, and let it be still for a moment.

Surround the egg of your problem with stillness. When thoughts or twitches come up, just observe them and let them pass, gently returning to the stillness. Let the stillness and peace penetrate the egg, healing whatever needs to be healed, returning it to wholeness. Just watch the egg and see what happens.

Any amount of time you can spend in stillness is healing. If you can spend one minute practicing being still—in traffic, between meetings, even in the restroom—the peace you create will gently begin to soften your hardest problems. The shells will begin to crack—hairline fractures will spread, and all unlike healing will fall away. Discord can't abide in harmony, agitation can't coexist with tranquility, uproar can't inhabit silence. If you practice being still, your problems no longer have a home, and will eventually start falling away.

{ 4 } Hugging Practice—Be Healing and Loving

The best way to practice being both healing and loving is to practice hugging. Why practice? Everyone knows how to hug, right?

We practice hugging to get better at healing and loving while we hug. The way in which we hug can make a big difference in whether the hug works its healing magic. Just the act of bringing two nervous systems together is likely to have beneficial effects for both, but when we practice really being there and know what the goal is, our hugs can become much more healing.

Imagine yourself hugging the most supportive person in your life. It could be a friend, a teacher, or a family member. See yourself being completely present—not thinking about something else—for the entire hug. Visualize your two nervous systems relaxing and equalizing, almost as if they were exchanging heat: warmth flowing into cold. Imagine both of you melting your frozen places: dissolving from stiff to soft, brittle to malleable, closed to open, prickly to comfortable, nervous to relaxed. Visualize exchanging compassion and understanding.

The next time you hug, you'll have this visualized practice to support you. You'll be able to see the hug as exchanging love and healing.

{ 5 } The Four Strengths—Be Healing and Strong

Healing begins with a conscious choice. Sometimes it's the choice to change unhealthy eating habits, or to begin exercising. Sometimes it's the choice to let unhealthy relationships fall away, or forgive old hurts. Sometimes it's simply the choice to remember To Be Healing, and bring that intention to your daily activities.

After you choose liberate yourself from any old, unhealthy pattern, you're going to have challenges. Some of them may require a lot of strength. Here are some exercises to build your strength and determination.

Exercise 1—Strength in the Body

Clench your fist, make a muscle with your bicep like Popeye, and say, "If anyone can do this, I can do this! If anyone can do this, I can do this!" If you can say it aloud, forcefully, your subconscious will hear it better and help you out. Do a pantomime of pushing away the heavy boulder that's the healing challenge in front of you. Tighten your muscles and really push, feeling the boulder slide out of your way in response to your strength.

Exercise 2—Strength in the Mind

Take a piece of paper and write down the answers to the following questions regarding your healing challenge.

What's already working well? Absolutely nothing negative or even mildly sarcastic belongs here. It's vital to your success to be energized by your progress, and to do more of what's already working.

What is my healing goal? Be crystal clear. What could you videotape that would let you know you've achieved the goal?

What are the benefits of achieving my healing goal? This is to strengthen your resolve to keep going. It will help you focus your mind on achieving success, versus getting mired in the challenge. Keep those benefits of success front and center in your mind.

Exercise 3—Strength in the Emotions

Bring your attention to your abdomen, just below your navel, and watch your breathing for a few breaths. Feel your emotional stability, like the trunk of a tree. Feel how the gale of your healing challenge, which may be whipping around your branches, can't move your solid, sturdy trunk. When you feel yourself getting frenzied, bring your attention back down to your abdomen and practice feeling emotionally grounded for a few breaths.

Exercise 4—Strength in the Spirit

Ask God, or the Universe, or the Divine: "What do You want me to do right now? Stay strong, or let go?" If the answer is truly to let go, then let go and don't look back.

But if the answer is to stay strong, then know that you have God on your side. Thank God for having already given you the strength to triumph over this challenge. God only gives us challenges that we already have the strength to handle, but the strength might be hidden at first. Say, "Thank You, God, for giving me all the strength I need to create a wonderful spiritual success in this healing. Help me discover it and use it to the best of my ability."

{ 6 } The Healing Oak—Be Healing and Balanced

In this exercise, we imagine the balance and healing power of a tree, and draw analogies to our own balance and healing power. We alternate between imagining the tree and visualizing ourselves like a tree.

Imagine a good, solid, sturdy oak tree. See it in your mind—stately, beautiful, symmetrical. Imagine the roots of the tree reaching deep into the earth below—solid, stable, dependable. Feel how the roots are in perfect health and balance, anchoring the tree, extracting the perfect nutrition from the soil, without stress or strain.

Now feel your own roots—all that feels solid and stable to you—your connection to nature, your friends, your ancestors, your teachers, your traditions, your sense of spirituality. Feel your roots anchoring you, grounding you, connecting you, nourishing you. See your roots taking in the perfect nutrition from their environment and feeding it to you, with ease and balance. Let all that is unlike balance and healing gently fall away.

Imagine the trunk of the oak emerging from the earth, reaching upward, and branching out in all directions. The trunk and branches provide form and structure to the tree. See the trunk solidly supporting the form of the tree in perfect balance and harmony, like the structure of a poem. The branches emerge and grow in just the right places to shape the tree into a masterpiece of symmetry and economy. All with perfect ease.

Now feel the trunk and branches of your life: what gives your life form and meaning? Your work, your hobbies, your passions, your relationships, your self-care. All your actions and choices form the branches of your life. Imagine them emerging effortlessly in just the right places at just the right times. They unfold and develop in their own perfect timing, in just the right way, guided by an infinitely wise and loving unseen power. Let all that is unlike balance gently fall away.

Imagine the oak's leaves fluttering in the breeze. See how they gratefully soak in light and air from the environment, inhaling and exhaling in perfect balance. They effortlessly dance with a passing storm, and patiently wait through the stillness of a draught. The leaves are born at just the right time and just the right place, they feed the tree their whole lives, ending with a flourish of color and falling to the ground to nourish the soil. All with perfect ease and grace.

Now imagine your own leaves—the ephemeral thoughts, feelings, experiences, and perceptions that flutter in the breezes of your life. Visualize them sprouting at just the right time and place for you. See how they take in just what you need from your environment, feeding you and nourishing you in perfect proportion, reacting to the storms and droughts of life with harmony and balance. At the perfect time, they finish up with a flourish of color and effortlessly return to the soil of your life experience. Imagine all that is unlike balance gently falling away.

{ 7 } The Pendulum of Courage—Be Healing and Courageous

Healing means repairing something that's broken. Where there is brokenness, there is always pain. Whether it's a physical illness, an emotional heartbreak, a mental stress, or a spiritual longing, the pain lets us know that something is not right. Something needs our attention.

The only way to heal is to give our attention to our pain. Allow it to be. Give it space to breathe. Hold it gently, with compassion and understanding.

Being present to our pain takes tremendous courage. To practice being healing and courageous, choose a small pain in your life. Maybe you have a headache, or tight shoulders, or a small resentment about an issue at work, or a little gripe about a situation at home. This shouldn't be anything very upsetting, just a small thing that you'd like to heal.

Tune into your breathing for one inhalation and exhalation. Feel how it feels going in and out your nose or mouth, going into your lungs, expanding and contracting your ribcage.

On the next breath, tune into your little pain. How does it feel? What are the bodily sensations, the mental sensations, the emotional sensations? Feel into it and probe it with your curious awareness.

Alternate between tuning into your breath and tuning into the pain. Swing your attention gently back and forth, like a pendulum. Watch how the pain slowly evolves. It may move, it may dissolve, it may change its character. Whatever happens is okay. The change is evidence that healing is taking place. Simply go back and forth between your breath and your little pain for as long as you like.

When we practice this way with our small, everyday pains, then we build up our courage to be mindfully present to our larger, deeper hurts. Every small hurt you heal in this way gently unravels old patterns, clearing the way for you to make new, joyful, peaceful patterns.

{ 8 } The Sigh of Relief—Be Healing and Grateful

When you want to manifest healing, try being grateful for the healing as if it had already happened.

Immense healing power is already present in our bodies and our minds. The body contains 50 trillion cells, each one of which knows just what it needs to take in and give back out in order to stay healthy. The mind can form more potential neural connections than the number of elementary particles in the known universe. When the body-mind system taps into this tremendous capacity to heal, miracles happen. So it is perfectly appropriate and honest to be grateful for the healing as if it had already occurred, because it's only a miracle away, and the body-mind system works miracles all the time.

To practice being grateful for the healing, imagine the feeling you'd have if the healing was complete. Feel a great sense of gratitude for the miracle, and place your hands in prayer position in front of your heart. Take a deep breath in, and let out a long, grateful sigh of relief. "Ahhhhhh! I am so happy and grateful for this healing. I am so grateful to be relieved of this problem. Ahhhhhh!"

{ 9 } The Teapot Handle—Be Healing and Bountiful

In order to be bountiful, you must be able to give freely. To give freely, you must feel whole and complete. So healing yourself allows you to create the feelings of bounteous abundance you seek.

Imagine that you have some dear friends coming over this evening, and you'd like to serve them some tea. But the handle on your teapot has broken off. In order to be able to share your tea with your friends, you have to repair the teapot by gluing the handle back on. Imagine gluing the handle back on now, so that your teapot is good as new, and imagine pouring your dear friends a steaming cup of aromatic tea.

What do you need to make whole in your life in order to be more bountiful? Pretend that broken piece in your life is the handle of a teapot, and visualize yourself gluing it back on so it's good as new. See the teapot whole and complete. Now imagine how your life looks with that part all fixed. See it perfectly the way you want it in order to be able to most joyfully and freely share your abundant blessings with those around you.

The more you practice seeing the healing and bounty in your life, the more of it there will be to see.

{ 10 } Waving the White Flag—Be Healing

In the end, we have to turn it all over to God. No matter how many exercises we do, no matter how clear our vision, no matter how pure our heart or complete our healing, we all must realize that we can't control our lives. The illusion of control is the source of a great deal of suffering.

The only way to heal from this ultimate brokenness is to surrender. "Let go and let God." Know that there's a power much greater than you, and turn yourself over to it. Only then will it be possible to heal the illusion of separateness between you and the Divine.

Imagine that you are carrying two heavy canvas shopping bags, one over each shoulder. The bags contain all your troubles, worries, doubts, fears, delusions, obsessions, and all the other psychological baggage that you habitually carry around. Imagine that you're so worn out from carrying these heavy burdens that you can't take another step. You take out a white flag, and summon enough strength to wave it, saying feebly, "I surrender, God. I give up. You can have it all back."

Just then, the Presence you know as God swoops in and takes the bags from you. You feel a whoosh of lightness and you know you are now completely supported. You spread your arms wide and lie back into a trust fall with absolute faith. God's arms are there to catch you, cradle you, hold you, carry you. You no longer need to carry your burdens, or anything else, for you have turned it all over to God.

May you be cradled in the Healing Hands of the Divine One, and may we all be granted complete healing.

Be an open channel—The To Be List Meditation

For water to flow freely through a pipe, the pipe must be clear of obstructions. For the energies on our To Be List to flow freely through our lives, our hearts and minds must be clear of obstructions.

The obstructions to letting these energies flow are our misconceptions. When we believe something about the world that is not true, it will block the natural flow of truth through our lives.

The misconception that causes the most painful obstruction is that we are separate. We mistakenly believe we are separate from each other, separate from all that surrounds us, and separate from the Divine. We sometimes forget about how connected we are to all other beings, living and non-living. When we forget, we feel bad, because we feel closed off from the world, isolated, and alone. We see others as obstacles and threats to our happiness.

To undo this misconception and re-open your channel, you need only look as far as your own breathing. Your breath is a simple and powerful reminder of your interconnectedness to the world.

Follow the journey of your breath: it starts as oxygen exhaled by a plant. Imagine the plant is far away, on the other side of the earth, and its oxygen is swept across the oceans and across mountains and plains to where you are. When you inhale, the air penetrates deeply into your lungs, working its way to the smallest little air sacks. Then your lung cells do their job and transport the oxygen into your blood cells. Your blood, with the oxygen inside, flows to your muscles.

So, the oxygen that was once in a plant on the other side of the earth is now deeply inside of you, part of your very muscle fiber. Your body transforms the oxygen into energy and carbon dioxide, which you then exhale. Then the carbon dioxide is inhaled by another plant and absorbed into its cells. Now you are in that plant! How many plants are you in? From how many plants have you come?

If you look closely, there is no separateness. The distinctions between outside and inside, before and after, you and me, become arbitrary. The light reaching your eyes from the sun was ninety-three million miles outside you just 8 minutes ago, but now it is *inside* you. The music composed by Mozart, who died long before you were born, is stored in the neurons in your brain. The teacher who believed in you, years ago and far away, passed their lessons to you, and through you, to the people you will influence.

We are all intimately connected with everything else. This is a mystical truth, and a physical fact.

When we open ourselves up to this reality of interconnectedness, when we dwell with this understanding, we become a clear and open channel. The energies of the To Be List can then flow within us, and we can Be Joyful, Be Free, Be Peaceful.

Everyone has feelings of separateness—it is the price of being human. But if we allow ourselves to live in the separateness for too long, we'll start to feel bad. Believing that we're separate from the rest of the universe will always impede the flow of the To Be List energies into our lives.

Instead, we want to keep our channel empty, ready to receive the energies we want. The To Be List Meditation that follows can serve to help you keep your channel open and remind you of the energies you wish to invite into your life.

The To Be List Meditation

You can do this meditation anywhere—waiting in line at the grocery store, at your desk between meetings, in the shower, or sitting quietly in your favorite chair.

You can do it in sixty seconds as a quick recharge. Or you can spend thirty minutes and use it to dramatically transform your energy level. If you spend even one minute with this meditation, you will find yourself in a considerably different place than when you started—you'll be able to easily hop back on Your To Be List. If you spend fifteen minutes a day with this meditation, it is guaranteed to change your life for the better.

The meditation is tied to your breathing. On each breath, you'll visualize being one of the Ten To Be's. Imagine a glowing light representing the To Be filling your heart, or your mind, body, or soul. As you breathe, you can silently say to yourself:

"[Breathe in] There is freedom... [Breathe out] in my heart." Feel your heart opened to freedom, opened by freedom, soaring with freedom.

"[In] There is joy... [out] in my heart." Feel your heart dancing with joy, smiling with joy, radiating with joy.

"There is peace... in my heart." Feel your heart peaceful like still waters, cool and calm, free and easy.

"There is love... in my heart." Feel your heart bathed in love, surrounded by love, radiating love.

"There is strength... in my heart." Feel your heart as strong, as powerful, as solid as a mountain.

"There is balance... in my heart." Feel your heart filled with the beauty of a sunset, the symmetry of a flower, the freshness of dew.

"There is courage... in my heart." Feel your heart surrounded with courage, supported by courage, backed by courage.

"There is gratitude... in my heart." Feel your heart filled with gratitude, overflowing with gratitude, surrendering to gratitude.

"There is bounty... in my heart." Feel your heart rich with bounty, bathed in prosperity, overflowing with abundant blessings.

"There is healing... in my heart." Feel your heart flowing with healing, receiving Divine healing, radiating healing.

Here are some variations for you to try. Use your intuition to select the one that feels right for you right now.

The One-Minute Recharger

Select a focus: heart, mind, body or soul. Then take one breath for each energy, like this:

"There is freedom... in my heart. "
"There is joy... in my heart."
"There is peace... in my heart." And so on.

The Five-Minute Makeover

Take four breaths for each energy, each with a different focus, like this:

"There is freedom... in my mind."
"There is freedom... in my body"
"There is freedom... in my spirit"
"There is freedom... in my heart."
"There is joy... in my mind." And so on.

The Thirty-Minute Transformation

Do the Five-Minute Makeover once all the way through, each time holding in mind a different recipient.

1) Yourself
2) A good friend
3) A neutral person (someone you don't know)
4) A difficult person
5) All life

This is based on the ancient Metta meditation sequence, and is proven to radically alter your level of compassion. The Metta mediation has been shown to physically make your brainwaves slower and more coherent. It also feels wonderful, and can lead you to transformative insights about the interconnected nature of reality.

When To Use the To Be List Meditation

There will be times that you want to use the energies on Your To Be List to revitalize your life and clarify your world view, but you just can't seem to find the energy you need. Let's say you are having a bad day at work. Intellectually, you know that if you felt grateful for your work you would feel better, but your work is producing such anxiety and worry that you can't seem to locate the energy of gratitude within yourself. Your gratitude is drowning in a sea of negative emotions.

Your To Be List Meditation is your way to throw a life preserver to your gratitude. You are saying: "Gratitude, I may not feel you right now, but I know you are there." You begin with Your To Be List Meditation in order to call out to your gratitude and ask for its help.

Soon enough, you will find your gratitude surfacing on the buoyancy of your breath. The waves of worry and anxiety will be calmed. The sea of emotions will no longer threaten you, they will become like a mirrored surface of a calm pond, reflecting the open channel of the sky.

Your breath is always with you, ready to support you in restoring Your To Be List energies.

Conclusion—
Be the Change

"We need to be the change we wish to see in the world."

— MAHATMA GANDHI

In his famous call to action, Gandhi summarizes for us the fundamental principle behind creating the kind of life we want for ourselves, and the kind of world we want for our children, and our children's children:

Be the change.

Most people long for happiness in their lives. They wish for peace. They hunger for meaning.

And then they wait. They wait for happiness to knock at their door. They wait for peace to descend from the heavens. They wait for meaning to dawn in their lives, as weary travelers wait for the sun to break on the horizon.

And unfortunately they will wait in vain. Because happiness is not outside of our homes and our hearts. Peace is not out of our reach. And the meaning of our lives is not hidden from us. We are not alone. We are not powerless. We are not in the dark.

The light of meaning is within us. Happiness, peace, and love are energies that vibrate through the world. And you and I are the channels through which the light of meaning flows. We are the vessels in which peace and happiness are made real, touchable, and visible to all who seek it.

Mahatma Gandhi knew this.

He went beyond feeling peaceful: he embodied the energy of Peace with all his being, and changed the world.

Martin Luther King, Jr. learned from the life of Gandhi. Dr. King went beyond feeling free: he embodied the energy of Freedom with all his being, and changed the world.

And Mother Teresa went beyond feeling loving: she embodied the energy of Love with all her being, and changed the world.

These great leaders all learned how to become experts at aligning their Being with the energies of peace, freedom, and love.

They had faith in the power of light over darkness. They worked diligently to open their hearts to the light of meaning. We are all beneficiaries of the great, open channels of their hearts. And the light that they shed upon the world continues to shine to this day.

You are made of the very same elements that these luminaries were made of. You are made of clay. You are made of stardust. You are made of light. The essential creative energies they channeled are energies that are available to you every moment of every day.

When we align our doing around our To Be's, we connect with the energy that underlies the To Be. Underneath "Be Peaceful" is the power of Peace. Underneath "Be Free" is the power of Freedom. Underneath "Be Loving" is the power of Love.

When we align ourselves with these underlying powers, it immediately pops us out of our egos into something bigger. It takes us out of our day-to-day cares, away from our minor complaints and our momentary discomforts. Peace, Freedom, and Love have the power to relieve us of our cares and discomforts.

All of the To Be's are energies that flow freely and are accessible to us, moment by moment. We just need to tune into their frequency, as we would tune into a radio station.

If you tune a radio to a particular frequency, you can hear what's on that radio station. You can carry your radio all around town, and no matter where you are, you will hear the music that is being broadcast. If your friends, your family, and your colleagues tune into the same station, then they will hear the same music as you. The radio waves are always there, but you can't hear the music they carry unless your radio is tuned to the right frequency.

If someone did not know that they could tune their radio, all they would hear is a terrible, brain-rattling static. They would cover their ears and scream: "This is terrible. It's nothing but noise. It makes no sense. I can't take it." That same person might see you driving by, tuned into your favorite station, singing and smiling. They might wonder how you could possibly be smiling or enjoying yourself when all they can hear is chaos: meaningless, garbled, unbearable noise. They do not know that you are hearing a symphony, or a gentle love song, or the harmony of many voices singing as one.

Your To Be's are not waves in an electromagnetic field, but more like waves in a spiritual field. Like radio waves, To Be waves carry energy, can travel through space and time, and have amplitude and frequency. You can't see radio waves, and you can't see To Be waves. But if you tune into the right frequency, you can hear the music.

Living by Your To Be List is the way you stay tuned to the right frequency. It allows you to embody the energies that you want in your life and which the world so desperately needs. And when others come close to you, they will hear the music that you are hearing. They will thrill to your symphony of your actions. They will delight to the gentle love song of your heart. They will tune to the harmony that rings out around you wherever you go.

You can be the change... *when you choose "To Be."*

Acknowledgements

The two of us could not have written this book by ourselves. We are indebted to many people who have offered us their talent, their wisdom, and their love.

The lessons in this book come from many spiritual traditions that we have studied over the years. We have written it so that you will find it accessible regardless of what spiritual path you walk or where you are on that path. We wish to acknowledge the many great teachers who have cast light on our paths. We are especially grateful for the spiritual teachings of the late Rabbi Abraham Joshua Heschel and the Venerable Thich Nhat Hanh. We have not only learned from the light of their words, but through the strength of their examples. Both of these remarkable men reached out from the rich faith traditions to understand the beliefs of others, to offer a compassionate hand, and to seek peace that embraces human diversity. Lauren would also like to thank her teacher and mentor from graduate school, Rabbi Nehemia Polen, for offering teachings that brought strength to her soul and light to her eyes.

We are deeply grateful to our spiritual mentors, Joan Borysenko and Gordon Dveirin for helping us stay open to the spiritual lessons that emerged for us as we created this book. If light flows through this book, it is because they helped us to keep our hearts and spirits open to that light—and to one another—as we wrote.

We are deeply grateful to James' mother Carol McMahon, for being a loving presence in our lives and in the lives or our children; and to James's father, Thomas McMahon and Lauren's parents, Ruth and Arnold Rosenfeld—whose bodies have passed from this world, but whose love and wisdom continues to touch our lives every day.

We are grateful for all our family and friends for the support they have offered though the years. Your loving support has allowed this work to manifest.

We are deeply grateful to the creative work of the To Be List team: our editor, Paula Felps; our cover designer, Patrick Scully; and our interior book designer, Jennifer Green.

And most of all, we are deeply grateful to our children: Mira, Alec, Tamar and Askar, who have taught us the importance of choosing who we wish To Be. Some people believe that parents form the shape of their children's lives. We know the opposite to be true. You have formed us into the shape of love. How can we ever repay you?

YourToBeList.com

Join Lauren and James online at YourToBeList.com, where you will find additional exercises, instructional videos, and the encouragement you need to stay on *Your To Be List* every day!

You can also follow us on Facebook and Twitter:
www.facebook.com/YourToBeList
www.twitter.com/YourToBeList

Made in the USA
Lexington, KY
20 April 2010